HELPING AFRICA HELP ITSELF: A GLOBAL EFFORT

HELPING AFRICA HELP ITSELF: A GLOBAL EFFORT

Anup Shah

Mason Crest Publishers

Philadelphia

Frontispiece: In the western Darfur region of Sudan, a young woman in the Internally Displaced Camp of Mourni receives cooking oil distributed by the United Nations World Food Program (WFP). Because of civil conflict in the country, more than a million Sudanese have been displaced from their homes and now rely on international donors for food, medical attention, and shelter.

Produced by OTTN Publishing, Stockton, New Jersey

Mason Crest Publishers
370 Reed Road
Broomall, PA 19008
www.masoncrest.com

First printing

1 3 5 7 9 8 6 4 2

Library of Congress Cataloging-in-Publication Data

Shah, Anup.
  Helping Africa help itself : a global effort / Anup Shah.
      p. cm. — (Africa: progress and problems)
  Includes bibliographical references and index.
  ISBN-13: 978-1-59084-923-1
  ISBN-10: 1-59084-923-X
  1. Economic assistance—Africa. 2. Africa—Economic conditions—1960- 3. Africa—Social conditions—
1960- 4. Africa—Politics and government—1960- I. Title.
HC800.S225 2007
338.91096—dc22
                              2006022237

TABLE OF CONTENTS

AFRICA: PROGRESS & PROBLEMS

AIDS AND HEALTH ISSUES

CIVIL WARS IN AFRICA

ECOLOGICAL ISSUES

EDUCATION IN AFRICA

ETHNIC GROUPS IN AFRICA

GOVERNANCE AND LEADERSHIP IN AFRICA

HELPING AFRICA HELP ITSELF: A GLOBAL EFFORT

HUMAN RIGHTS IN AFRICA

ISLAM IN AFRICA

THE MAKING OF MODERN AFRICA

POPULATION AND OVERCROWDING

POVERTY AND ECONOMIC ISSUES

RELIGIONS OF AFRICA

THE PROMISE OF TODAY'S AFRICA

by Robert I. Rotberg

oday's Africa is a mosaic of effective democracy and desperate despotism, immense wealth and abysmal poverty, conscious modernity and mired traditionalism, bitter conflict and vast arenas of peace, and enormous promise and abiding failure. Generalizations are more difficult to apply to Africa or Africans than elsewhere. The continent, especially the sub-Saharan two-thirds of its immense landmass, presents enormous physical, political, and human variety. From snow-capped peaks to intricate patches of remaining jungle, from desolate deserts to the greatest rivers, and from the highest coastal sand dunes anywhere to teeming urban conglomerations, Africa must be appreciated from myriad perspectives. Likewise, its peoples come in every shape and size, govern themselves in several complicated manners, worship a host of indigenous and imported gods, and speak thousands of original and five or six derivative common languages. To know Africa is to know nuance and complexity.

There are 53 nation-states that belong to the African Union, 48 of which are situated within the sub-Saharan mainland or on its offshore islands. No other continent has so many countries, political divisions, or members of the General Assembly of the United Nations. No other continent encompasses so many distinctively different peoples or spans such geographical disparity. On no other continent have so many innocent civilians lost their lives in intractable civil wars—12 million since 1991 in such places as Algeria, Angola, the Congo, Côte d'Ivoire, Liberia, Sierra Leone, and the Sudan. No other continent has so many disparate natural resources (from cadmium, cobalt, and copper to petroleum and zinc) and so little to show for their frenzied exploitation. No other continent has proportionally so many people subsisting (or trying to) on less than $1 a day. But then no other continent has been so beset by HIV/AIDS (30 percent of all adults in southern Africa), by tuberculosis, by malaria (prevalent almost everywhere), and by less well-known scourges such as schistosomiasis (liver fluke), several kinds of filariasis, river blindness, trachoma, and trypanosomiasis (sleeping sickness).

Africa is the most Christian continent. It has more Muslims than the Middle East. Apostolic and Pentecostal churches are immensely powerful. So are Sufi brotherhoods. Yet traditional African religions are still influential. So is a belief in spirits and witches (even among Christians and Muslims), in faith healing and in alternative medicine. Polygamy remains popular. So does the practice of female circumcision and other long-standing cultural preferences. Africa cannot be well understood without appreciating how village life still permeates the great cities and how urban pursuits engulf villages. Half if not more of its peoples live in towns and cities; no longer can Africa be considered predominantly rural, agricultural, or wild.

Political leaders must cater to both worlds, old and new. They and their followers must join the globalized, Internet-penetrated world even as they remain rooted appropriately in past modes of behavior, obedient to dictates of family, lineage, tribe, and ethnicity. This duality often results in democracy or at least partially participatory democracy. Equally often it develops into autocracy. Botswana and Mauritius have enduring democratic governments. In Benin, Ghana, Kenya, Lesotho, Malawi, Mali, Mozambique, Namibia, Nigeria, Senegal, South Africa, Tanzania, and Zambia fully democratic pursuits are relatively recent and not yet sustainably implanted. Algeria, Cameroon, Chad, the Central African Republic, Egypt, the Sudan, and Tunisia are authoritarian entities run by strongmen. Zimbabweans and Equatorial Guineans suffer from even more venal rule. Swazis and Moroccans are subject to the real whims of monarchs. Within even this vast sweep of political practice there are still more distinctions. The partial democracies represent a spectrum. So does the manner in which authority is wielded by kings, by generals, and by long-entrenched civilian autocrats.

The democratic countries are by and large better developed and more rapidly growing economically than those ruled by strongmen. In Africa there is an association between the pursuit of good governance and beneficial economic performance. Likewise, the natural resource wealth curse that has afflicted mineral-rich countries such as the Congo and Nigeria has had the opposite effect in well-governed places like Botswana. Nation-states open to global trade have done better than those with closed economies. So have those countries with prudent managements, sensible fiscal arrangements, and modest deficits. Overall, however, the bulk of African countries have suffered in terms of reduced economic growth from the sheer fact of being tropical, beset by disease in an enervating climate where there is an average of one trained physician to every 13,000 persons. Many lose growth prospects, too, because of the absence of navigable rivers, the paucity of ocean and river ports, barely maintained roads, and few and narrow railroads. Moreover, 15 of Africa's countries are landlocked, without comfortable access to relatively inexpensive waterborne transport. Hence, imports and exports for much of Africa are more expensive than elsewhere as they move over formidable distances. Africa is the most underdeveloped continent because of geographical and health constraints that have not yet been overcome, because of ill-considered policies, because of the sheer number of separate nation-states (a colonial legacy), and because of poor governance.

Africa's promise is immense, and far more exciting than its achievements have been since a wave of nationalism and independence in the 1960s liberated nearly every section of the continent. Thus, the next several decades of the 21st century are ones of promise for Africa. The challenges are clear: to alleviate grinding poverty and deliver greater real economic goods to larger proportions of people in each country, and across all 53 countries; to deliver more of the benefits of good governance to more of Africa's peoples; to end the destructive killing fields that run rampant across so much of Africa; to improve educational training and health services; and to roll back the scourges of HIV/AIDS, tuberculosis, and malaria. Every challenge represents an opportunity with concerted and bountiful Western assistance to transform the lives of Africa's vulnerable and resourceful future generations.

1 A TROUBLED CONTINENT

With its vast size and population, Africa holds great potential. The continent, which is second in size and population only to Asia, covers 11.6 million square miles (approximately 30 million sq km) of land. It is home to approximately 900 million people, 750 million of whom live in the region south of the Sahara Desert, or sub-Saharan Africa. The continent's 53 nations host a diversity of cultures and peoples, who speak more than 800 languages.

Africa is a continent of contrasts. It has some of the greatest lakes, wildlife, and ecosystems that nature can create, and yet has some of the most inhospitable and arid deserts. Endowed with rich, natural resources such as minerals, timber, and oil, Africa's promise is great. However, the land's wealth has been both a boon and a curse, attracting foreign powers that assumed control over the continent through colonial rule. Indeed, Africa still struggles to shake off the legacy of colonialism,

Children from Kenya's largest slum, Kibera, play in sewage. The quality of life in many African countries, as measured by life expectancy, education, and personal income, ranks at the lowest in the world.

which has left the continent mired in terrible poverty for decades.

POVERTY AND DISEASE

Today, almost all African countries suffer from many serious problems, with causes equally varied and often interconnected. Even as dictatorships that characterized many nations in their early post-colonial years give way to fledgling democracies, successful development has evaded many parts of the continent. According to the U.K. charity Oxfam, approximately 315 million Africans—more than the entire population of the United States—survive on less than one dollar per day. The majority (80 percent) of the African population lives on less than two dollars a day. Such low incomes mean that people cannot meet the basic needs for survival, such as food, health care, safe drinking water and sanitation, education, shelter, and clothing.

Africa is the only continent in the world to have grown poorer since 1979. From 1990 to 1999, poverty in the continent increased by 3 percent, whereas in all other areas of the world, poverty declined by about 7 percent. The number of people living in extreme poverty in sub-Saharan Africa has nearly doubled, from 164 million in 1981 to 315 million in 2001.

Africa's poverty has furthered problems such as high levels of illiteracy and disease. According to the United Nations (UN), a global organization that works to promote human rights and development, the majority of African countries can be described as "least developed countries," or LDCs. This socioeconomic development ranking is based on indicators such as average life expectancy, percentage of adult literacy, and gross national income (GNI, or the total value of goods and services produced within a country). Of the 50 countries identified by the United Nations as LDCs, 34 of them are in Africa.

Disease has run rampant in certain regions of Africa. The greatest killer has been AIDS (acquired immune deficiency syndrome), an incurable disease caused by the human immunodeficiency virus, or HIV. Other major diseases such as malaria and tuberculosis, which are rare in industrialized nations, are leading causes of death in sub-Saharan Africa. Because of serious health issues, particularly the HIV/AIDS pandemic, the average life expectancy for Africans has fallen to 49 years. Malnutrition (a lack of nutrients that the body needs to survive) and disease cause the deaths of one in six children before the age of five.

A BURDEN OF DEBT

Exacerbating the poverty in many African nations is debt—Africa owes billions of dollars to foreign countries and to international financial institutions such as the International Monetary Fund (IMF) and the International Bank for Reconstruction and Development (World Bank). In 1970 African debt stood at $11 billion. By 2002 that figure had risen to $295 billion.

Debt is a particularly heavy burden in sub-Saharan Africa's developing nations (defined as nonindustrialized countries in which people have a low standard of living and access to few goods and services). Of the 40 nations identified by the World Bank as heavily indebted poor countries (HIPCs), 34 are in Africa. Many LDCs do not have the money to repay their debts—in some cases the amount owed equals or surpasses the country's gross national income.

The existence of heavy debt in impoverished countries, sometimes referred to as "third world debt," has been an obstacle to growth and development. In order to make payments, debtor governments have been forced to drain resources from other areas such as health care and education. The effect on African society has been devastating: according to some estimates, since the late 1980s as many as 5 million children and vulnerable adults may have lost their lives in sub-Saharan Africa because of the debt burden of their governments. By 2015, the UN says, another 3 million children in the poorest countries of sub-Saharan Africa will die because of funding being channeled toward paying back debt rather than for health care.

HUMANITARIAN AND DEVELOPMENTAL AID

For many years, Africa has received large flows of humanitarian and developmental aid from countries outside the continent. Foreign aid has helped Africans through natural disasters such as extreme drought and floods, as well as manmade disasters such as warfare. Assistance has come from individual governments as bilateral aid (involving two countries) and multilateral aid (from several sources, commonly international organizations representing many countries, organizations, or groups).

Humanitarian aid relief consists of the basics needed for survival in times of crisis: food, shelter, clothing, and medical care. Such aid has been credited with saving the lives of millions, particularly when national authorities are unable to cope. The distribution of bilateral aid given in response to crises is often channeled through programs run by nongovernmental organizations, or NGOs (nonprofit groups or associations that operate outside the government, although they may receive funding from governments).

Relief-oriented NGOs deal strictly with humanitarian issues, working to alleviate suffering in times of severe drought, famine, or war. The largest humanitarian NGO is the International Red Cross and Red Crescent Movement. Others include CARE, World Vision, and Oxfam International, the latter of which is both relief-oriented and development-oriented.

Developmental aid is funding and technical help given to support economic development, with the long-term goal to alleviate poverty. In the United States, which distributes most of its bilateral aid through the U.S. Agency for International Development (USAID), goals for giving developmental aid have focused on promoting economic growth to reduce poverty, encouraging development of democratic systems, and mitigating global health problems.

FORMS OF FOREIGN AID

Some nations have addressed problems of poverty and debt by obtaining outside economic assistance from developed countries and multilateral institutions such as the World Bank and IMF. Such assistance may be in the form of grants, loans, or concessional loans.

In 2003 food aid from the United States bound for drought-stricken Ethiopia is delivered at Djibouti Town, in the nearby country of Djibouti. That year the Food and Agricultural Organization of the United Nations announced that approximately 11.3 million Ethiopians required food assistance.

Grants are funding given without requiring repayment. On occasion, cash grants may be given to a government to support its service debts; purchase specific goods; or provide for economic, education, or health programs. In an effort to promote economic development at the community level in impoverished countries, grants may also be given to microcredit organizations—groups that give very small loans to very poor, unemployed individuals who are trying to establish businesses. Such microentrepreneurs would normally not be able to receive any financial support through traditional banking services.

Among the many goals of the U.S. Agency for International Development (USAID) is the promotion of economic growth in low-income countries. Entrepreneur Mthembeni Mkhize benefited from the USAID program SAIBL, or South African International Business Linkages, which helped him connect with international companies and make additional sales. Strong growth of Mkhize's company has resulted in the creation of more jobs.

Loans require repayment, at established interest rates and schedules. Much of the foreign aid given as loans to Africa has typically come from the IMF and World Bank. Sometimes very poor countries receive concessional loans, which are loans given to countries at favorable terms—with lower interest rates and longer repayment periods than usual.

Foreign aid may also come in the form of food commodities or equipment such as generators or computers. Food donations may be considered humanitarian aid, when given in response to a crisis such as famine or warfare. Or food could be part of developmental aid, when used to encourage people to take part in health or education programs.

When equipment is given as developmental aid, it is usually combined with technology transfer (training on how to use the donated items). Other training aid may come from volunteer or paid schoolteachers, health workers, or law enforcement personnel. In some cases, foreign aid provides consultants who give governments or private sector organizations advice on program or policy reforms.

Aid given in the form of debt relief, or the forgiveness of existing debt, has benefited some nations in Africa. At various summits of the world's eight industrialized nations, known as the G8 (Canada, France, Germany, Italy, Japan, Russia, the United Kingdom, and the United States)—and at other international forums—leaders of wealthy countries have announced debt relief packages for the poorest nations.

INTERNATIONAL ASSISTANCE

The United Nations is one of the major providers of emergency relief and long-term foreign aid assistance. Each year

Medicines needed to treat diseases worsened or brought on by malnutrition are unloaded at Niamey, in Niger, in July 2005. In addition to food relief in times of famine, such medications are needed to help save lives.

the World Food Program (WFP) provides approximately two thirds of the world's emergency food supply, and the Office of the United Nations High Commissioner for Refugees (UNHCR) assists more than 20 million people worldwide. Many recipients of relief are in Africa.

Other UN organizations working to address some of Africa's problems are the World Health Organization (WHO), the Food and Agricultural Organization (FAO), and the United Nation's Children's Fund (UNICEF). The United Nations Development Program (UNDP) is involved not only in providing emergency relief during disasters but also in rehabilitation efforts, sometimes designing programs and directing donor aid.

In September 2000 the member states of the United Nations set eight objectives that, if met, would improve the standard of living by the year 2015 for people in developing countries. The international community signed on to the UN Millennium Development Goals (MDGs), which call for countries to meet deadlines for objectives such as eradicating extreme poverty; reducing child mortality; and combating AIDS, malaria, and

UNITED NATIONS MILLENNIUM DEVELOPMENT GOALS

1. Eradicate extreme poverty and hunger
2. Achieve universal primary education
3. Promote gender equality and empower women
4. Reduce child mortality
5. Improve maternal health
6. Combat HIV/AIDS, malaria and other diseases
7. Ensure environmental sustainability
8. Develop a global partnership for development

Source: http://www.un.org/millenniumgoals/goals.html, accessed 2006.

Reports on the effort to meet the United Nation's Millennium Development Goals are discussed at the September 2005 UN General Assembly. Many analysts question whether the eight objectives will be met in Africa by the 2015 deadline.

other diseases. The MDGs have inspired numerous international health initiatives and other efforts to help the world's poor.

In addition to foreign aid donations from the governments of richer countries, over the past decades humanitarian and developmental aid for Africa has come from the private sector, which includes global institutions, generous and concerned citizens, churches, universities, and companies. Global funds to help fight diseases such as AIDS and malaria have been boosted by the philanthropy of some of the richest people, countries, and companies in the world.

With all this assistance, why do problems in African nations persist? Why is there so much poverty? Have those forms of assistance helped, not made a difference, or even made things worse? Are the efforts being made truly enabling Africans to help themselves?

EXPLOITATION AND DEBT

Over the centuries European countries have looked to Africa as a source of labor and raw materials. Both the transatlantic slave trade and establishment of colonialism illustrate European exploitation of the continent.

LEGACY OF THE SLAVE TRADE

Between 1500 and 1900, more than 15 million Africans were shipped under inhumane conditions to the Americas, where they toiled as slaves on plantations and in mines. Millions more perished in wars and conflicts caused for the sole purpose of taking slaves, or died during the long, brutal passage overseas.

The slave trade devastated Africa. It drained the continent of its laborers and bred mistrust among members of the indigenous communities, reducing their ability to join together against foreign incursion in their land. Although the transatlantic slave trade officially ended in 1888, when the last country in the Western hemisphere—Brazil—outlawed slavery, the practice continued to affect Africa in the years that followed.

LEGACY OF COLONIALISM

From the late 1800s until the early 1900s, in a period referred to as the Scramble for Africa, European powers partitioned the continent among themselves in efforts to gain control over the region's many natural resources, particularly its diamonds and gold. At the Berlin Conference of 1884–85 European nations resolved their claims to African land by a treaty. By 1914, most of Africa had been colonized—there were 40 European colonies and protectorates in Africa, with boundaries that had been determined by Europe and European interests, not African ones.

During the late 1800s, Western Europe became very powerful, capable of global conquest, successful industrialization, and advances in many fields. To the majority of Europeans, these successes and advances confirmed their superiority over other peoples, an attitude reflected in the writings produced at that time. For many Europeans, the belief in differences in abilities based on race explained why Western European nations had successfully developed and industrialized, while other societies did not. Members of Western civilization considered their society the most advanced of the world.

Such views served a number of purposes. For businesses looking to expand into new territories, the belief in European superiority served to justify colonial expansion into other people's lands. Christian missionaries and others from Europe saw Africa as a "dark continent" in need of Christian light, and its people as savage or primitive, in need of being civilized. European missionaries viewed the people of the continent in a condescending manner, treating them much like naïve children requiring guidance from parents. Similarly, the idea of racial

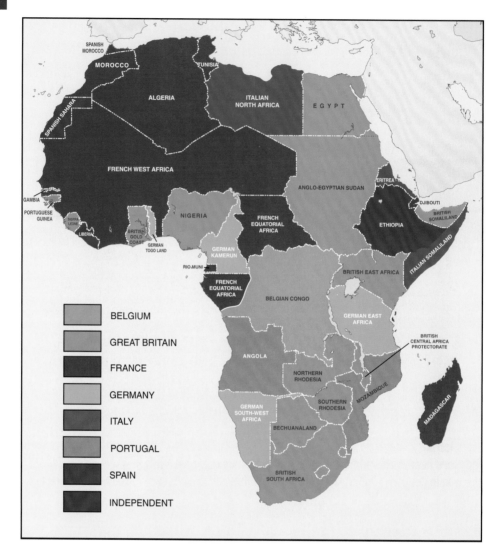

During the late 1800s the Western European powers began dividing Africa among themselves. By 1914 their "Scramble for Africa" had produced the political divisions shown here.

superiority, which had justified the practice of slavery during the 1700s and 1800s, further legitimized the right of Europeans to take over African lands.

During colonial rule Europeans supported the construction of schools and churches, building of roads, and the establishment of massive agricultural plantations throughout Africa. Large settlements of Europeans arose in parts of eastern and southern Africa, as whites were encouraged to live on the continent.

Christian missionaries had established a presence in many parts of Africa by the time colonialism ended, and were responsible for the founding of numerous medical clinics and schools. In this 1963 photograph, children in southern Sudan take part in a religious procession at a Roman Catholic mission.

INDEPENDENCE AND DECOLONIZATION

After African rebellions against colonial rule intensified during the 1950s and 1960s, many European powers granted independence to their colonies. With decolonization, most African countries became self-governing. Unfortunately, during the 1960s and beyond, the achievement of independence brought mixed results.

Under colonialism, European administrators had emphasized agricultural and mineral production. Rather than develop major manufacturing businesses that would have competed with industries back home, colonial rulers used Africa to provide raw materials for industries in the West. As a result, when African countries gained independence, they did not have the factories and skilled workers of an industrial society.

In addition, many countries lacked the infrastructure (transportation, electricity supplies, water access) required to meet the needs of modern societies and promote development. The continent's railways had been built to service European interests, leading from mines to urban centers. There was no network of roads. Africa's infrastructure was suitable for exporting resources and materials out of the continent, rather than for connecting cities and regions within the continent.

As colonial administrations officially withdrew from some African countries, they left in place governments and power

The lack of an effective transportation network, especially paved roads, has long hindered Africa's economic development and remains a problem today. This dirt path in the Democratic Republic of the Congo is typical of the transportation infrastructure in that country, where a 50-mile trip by car can take up to seven hours.

structures that favored European interests. For the most part, after independence African nations continued to export their raw materials and resources mainly to Europe. The newly independent countries had little opportunity to diversify their economies and build successful local manufacturing industries.

The new nations had European-imposed artificial borders, which had been established with no regard to the approximately 10,000 cultural and ethnic groups lying within their boundaries. Under colonial rule, these groups had had little or no opportunity to form political alliances. With independence, old antagonisms and personal ambitions surfaced, causing much instability as ethnic groups began fighting one another.

Many African nations found themselves starting their new independent life from a very disadvantaged position. Leaders inherited nations with severe economic and major developmental problems, including vast illiteracy and mass poverty. There were few experienced administrators or public officials to run government programs. The lack of roads and railways hindered socioeconomic development: the ill could not easily access medical care, and farmers and businesses could not easily bring products to market.

In addition, many newly independent nations were forced to assume huge debts that had been incurred during colonial rule. These heavy debt burdens were a serious impediment to economic development.

THE COLD WAR

In the two decades following independence, approximately 40 successful military coups took place, in which governments were overthrown and dictators came into power. The dream of successful independence for Africa withered, as new nations evolved into dictatorships.

Many African dictators were supported by superpowers—either the United States or the Soviet Union—that were locked in an ideological conflict of capitalism versus communism. Known as the Cold War, this conflict caused much political instability in Africa, as the capitalist United States and communist Soviet Union supported regimes—typically dictatorships—that were friendly to their interests.

As the two powers and their allies vied for influence in the continent, they lent money, food, and arms to African governments. Both the United States and the Soviet Union saw the giving of foreign aid as a way to further their own political objectives: to attract African countries away from the other superpower's influence. For the United States, giving foreign aid to African nations was seen as a way to encourage economic growth and further capitalism.

GROWING DEBT

African countries accepted foreign aid from the superpowers in the form of grants and loans, often made at high interest rates. Other Western governments gave money to Africa, as well. In 1964 the level of aid to sub-Saharan Africa was more than $1 billion.

In efforts to speed their economic development, many newly independent African countries were encouraged to base their agricultural economies on just a few cash crops, such as tea, coffee, cotton, or cocoa. However, in the 1980s the global economy slowed and prices for cash crops fell. Because Africa's developing countries were dependent on just a few export commodities, their economies faltered and making loan repayments became increasingly difficult.

In 1970 Africa's external debt (the amount that governments owe creditors from outside the country) was just under $11 billion. By 2002, Africa's debt was $295 billion. A number of factors worked together to exacerbate the debt problem in Africa: increased borrowing, high interest rates, government inefficiency and corruption, and the need to repay existing debt.

BORROWING

During the late 1970s and early 1980s, the organization of the petroleum-exporting countries (OPEC) increased the price of oil, an act that had an impact on the world economy. Soaring prices contributed to a global recession, and the market demand for commodities from developing nations began to slow. With reduced trade, developing nations saw their export income fall.

As poor countries grew increasingly poor, Western banks and governments offered more loans. In many cases, the African governments took out new loans so they could make payments on the old debts.

HIGH INTEREST RATES

On a plantation in 1960s Angola, coffee beans are spread out to dry. After achieving independence, many newly independent African nations continued to base their economies on agriculture, producing such cash crops as coffee, cocoa, and cotton.

Governments had to pay back not only the principal of their loans but also the interest, which sometimes was charged at very high rates. In some cases poor countries had to pay in currencies other than their own, and under unfavorable exchange rates. Compounding interest led to a situation in which many governments had paid off the principal of their loan but still owed a great deal of money because of interest.

On the website of the Jubilee Debt Coalition (a partnership of antipoverty groups in the United Kingdom calling for cancellation of debts in developing countries), President Olusegun Obasanjo of Nigeria commented on the debt his country faced in 2000. "All that we had borrowed up to 1985 or 1986 was around $5 billion," he explained, "and we have paid about $16 billion yet we are still being told that we owe about $28 billion. That $28 billion came about because of the injustice in the foreign creditors' interest rates. If you ask me what is the worst thing in the world, I will say it is compound interest."

CORRUPTION

Through corruption, mismanagement, or both, many African dictators incurred massive debt within their nations. Some of these leaders embezzled money, which they hid in foreign bank accounts or spent on lavish lifestyles. (Some economists estimate that 40 percent of Africa's private wealth is invested outside the continent, either by corrupt dictators who have diverted money into private accounts or by the wealthy, who have invested in foreign banks or property). Rather than spending money on programs and infrastructures that would benefit their people, African ruling elites used funds to increase personal power and to purchase military equipment from the West, the former Soviet Union, and other major arms producers.

In many nations government corruption ran rampant. Officials in charge of awarding contracts for the extraction of their country's natural resources were known to accept bribes from foreign multinational corporations and grant access at terms that did not necessarily benefit the nation or its citizens. Similarly, corruption played a role in how leaders with personal or political agendas used—and misused—foreign aid.

For example, former dictator of the Democratic Republic of the Congo Mobutu Sese Seko was supported by the United States when he took over the government in a military coup in 1965. He subsequently used U.S. foreign aid and military assistance to strengthen his political power, and even brutally suppress his own people. For three decades Mobutu plundered his nation's economy and directed revenues from state-owned companies into his pockets and those of his closest allies. His family amassed a fortune, while the nation accumulated debt amounting to some $12 billion. Although the corrupt dictator was overthrown in 1997, the successor government headed by Joseph Kabila has also been accused of corruption and misuse of aid, ranging from the diversion of taxes by local militias to the interception of food aid.

After coming to power in a 1965 military coup, General Joseph-Désiré Mobutu ruled as president of Zaire for 32 years. Later referred to as Mobutu Sese Seko, the former dictator of today's Democratic Republic of the Congo misused foreign aid and diverted money to accumulate vast personal wealth at the expense of his people.

REPAYMENT OF EXISTING DEBT

A vicious cycle evolved for debtor nations. As they devoted large portions of their government budgets to debt repayment, their economic growth slowed, and so they required more loans and assistance. Many countries spent 5 to 25 percent of their entire government revenue on debt servicing; some spent as much as 25 to 40 percent of their budgets.

Since the 1970s African nations have paid back approximately $550 billion in principal and interest on $540 billion worth of loans. Because this money went to debt servicing, less funding was available for health, education, infrastructure, and other elements of societal development that could have contributed to political stability in these countries.

CONDITIONAL FOREIGN AID

In order to receive grants, loans, or debt relief, countries sometimes must meet specific requirements set by the donor. Placing restrictions on aid invites criticism that the aid is being given to advance the interests of the donor, not necessarily the recipient. On the other hand, certain reforms that have been tied to developmental aid may help promote economic, political, and social improvement in countries with governments dominated by corruption.

TIED AID

In some cases development assistance is given with the condition that the recipient country use the money to buy goods and services only from the donor country. Referred to as tied aid, this kind of donation benefits the donor nation because money is pumped back into its economy. However, because the products and services purchased from the donor country can cost much more than if purchased elsewhere, the

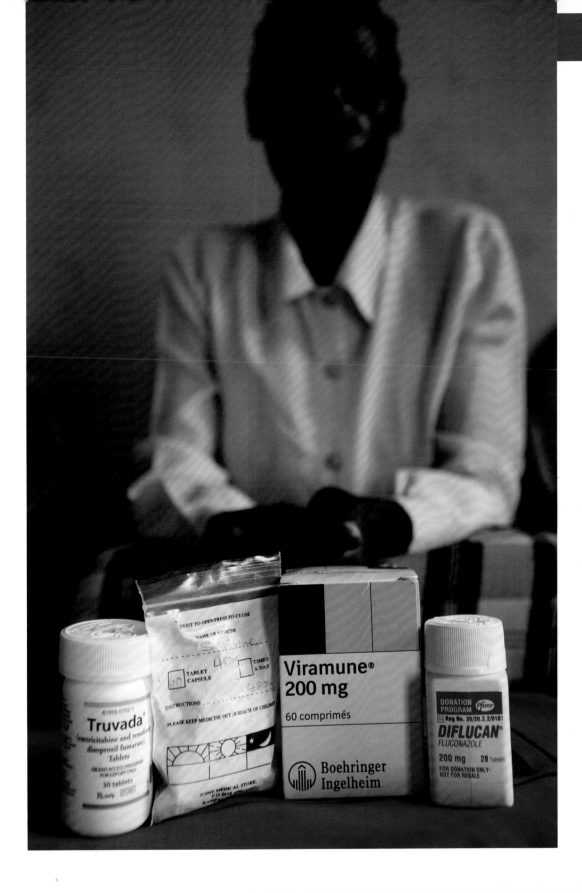

recipient may not obtain the full value of the aid package. With tied aid, aid money is invested outside the recipient country and not within its domestic markets.

According to the UN Economic Council for Africa, tied aid can cut the value of an aid package from 25 to 40 percent. Much of the foreign aid given by Canada, the United States, Germany, Japan, and France to developing countries requires that the money be used to buy products originating in those donor countries. However, more than 90 percent of aid given by Norway, Denmark, the Netherlands, and the United Kingdom is untied.

REQUIRING POLITICAL CHANGE

Because of Africa's historical problems with the misuse of aid, donors may require that recipient nations make political changes in order to receive funding. Government reforms may include increasing support for democratic institutions, eliminating corruption, and increasing government transparency (improving accessibility to information about government practices). Because good governance and transparency have been tied to economic growth, donor countries have strongly encouraged the development of democracies in poor countries.

Donor countries have also diverted, cut, or reconsidered awarding aid in order to influence the political actions of African governments. For example, in December 2005 Sweden diverted $5 million in promised aid from the Ugandan government because of the arrest of a main opposition party leader. Also concerned about human rights abuses and the slow progress toward democracy in Uganda, Great Britain cut $27.6 million in aid at the same time.

REQUIRING ECONOMIC CHANGE

Beginning in the 1970s many conditional loans made to Africa were from international financial institutions, such as the World

Bank and the International Monetary Fund. These institutions were established in 1944, toward the end of the Second World War, to help Europe rebuild. The original goal of the IMF was to promote steady growth and employment in countries by providing loans to economies in crisis and helping to stabilize exchange rates. Eventually, the roles of the IMF and World Bank changed to that of lenders and providers of economic assistance to developing countries.

During the late 1970s and 1980s the threat of defaults on loans led the IMF and World Bank to step in with loans for African countries. Most funding went to massive development projects, such as dams and highways, but it also went toward military and armament funding. Most aid consisted of loans that required recipients to meet conditions established by the IMF Structural Adjustment Programme (SAP).

SAP policies were based on an economic ideology called neoliberalism. Neoliberal policies require cutbacks in state expenditures, the opening up of markets for foreign competition and investment, and the privatization of many state functions and assets. Under neoliberalism, the private sector—and not the government—provides services such as health and education, in the belief that the drive for profits and the competition among private organizations makes them more efficient than public ones. By increasing efficiency, profits will increase. As a result wealth will circulate within the country and increase.

Neoliberal policies also encouraged countries to concentrate their national economies on one or two export commodities, with the assumption that this focus would allow the nation to develop expertise and thus excel at producing those particular items. The export income would allow the country to import any other needed commodities. As a result of following this policy, many African countries became dependent on just one or two products as sources for their national income.

In order to qualify for new World Bank and IMF loans, developing countries were required to restructure their economies, tighten up on spending, and follow austerity measures. Many economists believed that these reforms would generate more government income, while decreasing expenses, and thus promote future economic growth.

SAP conditions typically required nations to make the following reforms:

✳ Reduce government expenditures for social programs. By following an austerity policy, in which the role of the state in providing government services in health, education, and social care is reduced, the resulting reduction in public spending would provide the money needed to pay back creditors. In some cases, this meant imposing user fees for basic services.

✳ Privatize public assets by selling state-owned operations and enterprises to private firms and individuals.

✳ Open up the economy to foreign investment, by removing or reducing existing standards and regulations (such as environmental standards and financial regulations). Increase "flexibility" in the labor market (that is, make it easier for businesses to hire and fire people).

✳ Liberalize trade by lifting import and export restrictions (with the objective to increase exports and reduce imports, in order to improve the nation's balance of payments).

✳ Devalue overvalued currencies, balance national budgets, and remove state-mandated price controls and state subsidies.

As the Cold War was drawing to a close in the late 1980s African countries could no longer look to the Soviets for economic assistance. Many countries had no choice but to accept conditions as set forth by SAP policies. However, incorporation of these economic policies had a number of negative effects.

IMPACT OF STRUCTURAL ADJUSTMENT PROGRAMME POLICIES

SAP policies were supposed to help African nations achieve price stability and economic growth. However, the privatization of public enterprises and imposition of user fees, as required by SAP policies, caused the prices for basic services, such as water, health, and education, to go up. Similarly, the removal of subsidies that helped keep prices low for basics such as food made

Austerity measures imposed by Structural Adjustment Programmes have required African governments to reduce their budgets, often by making cuts in health and social services programs and by eliminating public health services.

many products more expensive. Rising prices for food and medical care hurt the poor the most.

Instead of promoting economic growth, SAP policies have been linked to a decline in the gross domestic product (GDP, the value of all final goods and services produced within a country in a given period of time) of many African countries. Economist Ha Joon Chang reported in his book, *Kicking Away the Ladder* that between 1960 and 1980, sub-Saharan Africa had on average 1.5 percent of GDP growth per year. But when SAP policies were in place between 1980 and 1999 there was negative growth of -0.7 percent of GDP per year, on average. World Bank figures for the period between 2000 and 2004 show that the average GDP growth in sub-Saharan Africa was 3.86 percent. While this sounds good, the overall 25 years since 1980 indicate that the rate of growth for sub-Saharan Africa actually declined, compared to 1960–1980, to an average growth rate of just 0.21 percent.

Still, many African states have also been part of the problem, says political science professor Nicolas Van de Walle. In his book *African Economies and the Politics of Permanent Crisis, 1979–1999*, he notes that in a number of African countries political leaders initially were hostile to reform. Because they feared losing or diluting their power, some leaders actively tried to evade reform. It was only later, when they saw they could benefit from the reform prescriptions, that they selectively implemented changes. As a result, SAP policies and accompanying Western aid helped them maintain power, while insulating them from most public protest.

The resulting political instability, however, was not conducive to the economic reform that most economists believed was required. Furthermore, Van de Walle argues, some leaders also used aid to avoid their own responsibilities in service provision and as a result lacked the incentive to proceed with needed reforms. Van de Walle notes that over a 20-year period "Africa underwent rapid political change" as "democratization and political liberalization transformed African politics, with the introduction of multiple parties, regular elections, a free press, and an explosion of civic associations." Unfortunately, he notes, lending institutions neglected to address this area when issuing loans, by commonly giving loans to dictators.

Similarly, the SAP requirement to liberalize trade did not help Africa trade its way out of poverty. Instead, the opposite occurred, and poverty increased. Many African countries had focused their national exports on just a few mineral and agricultural products, such as diamonds, gold, platinum, exotic woods, cocoa, or coffee. When nations have only a few commodities

Because many African countries have agriculture-based economies, they suffered when the international prices for their cash crops declined. Today, anti-globalization activists, such as these Ugandan farmers demonstrating in Johannesburg, South Africa, charge that SAP policies increased poverty by forcing developing countries to compete in an unfair international trade market.

available for export, rather than an assortment of products from a diverse domestic industry, their economies can be significantly affected by global market demands and fluctuations. Falling commodity prices require them to export more goods, contributing to deflated world prices (which benefits consumers in wealthier countries, but not the producers in developing countries).

The export of goods such as coffee and lumber may bring in revenue, but the problem of unequal trade results because most of Africa's major exports are unprocessed goods. They cost much less than the processed goods (which require more labor) that African nations import from industrialized nations. In his 2002 book *Global Problems and the Culture of Capitalism* Richard Robbins explains:

> A country that exports lumber but does not have the capacity to process it must then re-import it in the form of finished lumber products, at a cost that is greater than the price it received for the raw product. The country that processes the materials gets the added revenue contributed by its laborers.

That is, the amount of money circulated through an economy of a nation that exports processed products is far greater than the amount circulated in countries in which raw or unprocessed materials are exported.

Income from exports was also affected by SAP policies. Nations told to peg their currencies to the more stable dollar found that dollar fluctuations reduced the value of their exports, sometimes making it harder to pay off debts. Poor countries found they had to export even more commodities to raise enough foreign exchange for debt repayment.

By concentrating on similar cash crops and liberalizing trade so quickly, poor countries found themselves in price wars with each other, or in a "race to the bottom." Protests against IMF policies erupted as antipoverty activists criticized Structural Adjustment Programme policies for failing the people they were

A worker crafts wood into a chair in a South African furniture factory. Most lumber in Africa is exported to foreign markets, where it is sold and made into finished products. Such processed goods may be re-imported by African nations, but at much higher costs to African consumers than if they had been produced locally.

supposed to help and for contributing to increased poverty. A June 2005 article posted on the website of the nongovernmental organization Christian Aid is highly critical of SAP policies; it estimates that free trade policies forced on sub-Saharan Africa over a period of 20 years as a condition of receiving aid and debt relief has worsened the region's economy by $272 billion.

For many poor countries, liberalized trade has resulted in a massive growth in imports with only an insignificant increase in exports. And reliance on a narrow range of agricultural and mineral products has left many African countries to suffer from declining export earnings. Africa is the only continent in recent years to have experienced declining percentages of world trade.

CRITICISMS OF SAP POLICIES

Some critics of Structural Adjustment Programme economic conditions say the reforms give the donor too much control over aid funds, thus stifling the ability for the recipient to make the best use of aid. In his book *Globalization and Its Discontents*, former World Bank chief economist Joseph Stiglitz criticized World Bank and IMF policies, including those of the Structural Adjustment Programme, which he once helped promote. Stiglitz noted how the IMF demanded that countries open up and liberalize their financial and banking sectors before they were ready to do so.

Both Stiglitz and the president of Ethiopia, which is dependent largely upon rural farming, believed that privatizing that country's banks should not take place because they were not sufficiently developed to compete against Western banking giants. Ethiopia resisted privatization because of what had happened to its neighbors. For example, the IMF's insistence on financial market liberalization in Kenya led to 14 banking failures in that country in 1993 and 1994.

In Tanzania, former president Julius Nyerere told *New Internationalist Magazine* in 1999 that the financial restrictions imposed by the IMF and World Bank were to blame for Tanzania's decline. Nyerere described how his country had improved following independence in the 1960s, when 86 percent of the adult population was illiterate and there were only 2 trained engineers and 12 doctors. By the time he left office in 1985, Nyerere explained, nearly every child was in school; the literacy rate had reached 91 percent; and thousands of engineers, doctors, and teachers had been trained.

But during the 1990s the country deteriorated dramatically. In 1988 Tanzania's per-capita income was $280; by 1998 its per-capita income had been halved, to just $140. When Nyerere was questioned by World Bank officials as to what went wrong, he responded that Tanzania had done everything required of it by the IMF and World Bank. He blamed ten years of following IMF and World Bank policies for the 63 percent decline in school enrollment and the loss of health and other social services in the country.

In a 2006 article in *Yale Economic Review* economist Jeffrey Sachs notes that World Bank and IMF policies calling upon nations to "privatize, get government out of the markets, reduce the number of civil servants . . . had no [positive] effect at all." He stated that despite being in place in Africa for 20 years, SAP policies did not promote economic development in Africa.

Some analysts also criticize World Bank and IMF policies as favoring the rich nations over the poor. A major issue is the imposition of various conditions that low-income nations must agree to follow in order to obtain loans. In some cases, conditions require countries to pass certain laws or to adhere to rigid timetables stating specific goals that must be accomplished within particular time periods. The leaders of affected countries often come to resent such conditions, which are seen as interfering in their internal affairs and reducing their political sovereignty.

GHANA'S ECONOMIC IMPROVEMENT

For many years, the IMF, World Bank, and others have pointed to Ghana as an example of successful Structural Adjustment Programme policies. However, professor of sociology Walden Bello believes otherwise. In his 1994 book *Dark Victory: The United States and Global Poverty*, Bello explains that Ghana's external debt rose from $1.7 billion in early 1983 to $3.5 billion in 1990. At the same time, the author stated, Ghana's economy weakened as "import liberalization" caused the loss of hundreds

Some analysts credit Structural Adjustment Programme policies adopted by Ghana in the early 1980s for improving the country's economy. However, economic reforms forced people to pay for services previously subsidized by the state such as clean water, a primary school education, and basic health care. SAP policies have been blamed for reducing the quality of life and intensifying poverty for many Ghanaians, particularly those living in rural areas.

of jobs in the textile industry and the closing of local manufacturing industries.

While Ghana has seen economic growth figures rise in recent years, critical issues still remain, such as the rise in infant mortality and malnutrition. In addition, a 2005 report by the United Nations Development Program (UNDP) notes that inequality in Ghana is very high. Although the incidence of poverty in the capital city of Accra is just 2 percent, in the rural savannah (which accounts for one-fifth of the population), it reaches 70 percent. Although Ghana has shown signs of economic growth in recent years, the UNDP report notes that overall human development (as measured by indicators such as life expectancy, adult literacy, and school enrollment) has declined.

PROMOTING ECONOMIC DEVELOPMENT

Although economic decline appears to have accompanied the use of Structural Adjustment Programme loans in Africa, monetary institutions continue to prefer conditional aid under the belief that it keeps recipient governments free from corruption. Many donor nations and international financial institutions continue to look to SAP policies as the long-term solution to the region's poverty. However, they also recognize that reducing poverty in Africa means addressing the heavy debt burdens of low-income nations and providing sufficient developmental aid.

DEBT RESTRUCTURING AND DEBT RELIEF

In 1996 the IMF and World Bank launched a new program to help extremely poor nations handle their debt problems. Called the Heavily Indebted Poor Countries Initiative (HIPC), it was established so that the World Bank, the IMF, and other international financial institutions could identify and subsequently work with the world's poorest nations identified as carrying unmanageable debt.

In 2001 there were 17 countries, mostly heavily indebted poor countries, that received $25.6 billion by having debt rescheduled—that is, agreements were made that changed terms and conditions of payment. Critics note that restructuring does not really help least developed countries, however, because it only delays the payment of debt for LDCs but does little to help solve the problem on how to pay for it.

In 2005 the HIPC Initiative was supplemented by a new plan called the Multilateral Debt Relief Initiative (MDRI), in which three multilateral institutions—the IMF, the International Development Association of the World Bank, and the African Development Fund—provide 100 percent debt relief for qualified countries. In June 2006 the World Bank announced that MDRI had approved debt cancellation for 19 HIPC countries, most of them in Africa, effective July 1, 2006. An additional 21 world countries were potentially eligible to have their debt cancelled through the initiative as well.

To be considered for assistance under the HIPC initiative, notes the IMF website, "countries must (1) face an unsustainable debt burden . . . ; (2) establish a track record of reform and sound policies through IMF- and World Bank-supported programs; and (3) have developed a Poverty Reduction Strategy Paper (PRSP) through a broad-based participatory process."

Poverty Reduction Strategy Papers, or PRSPs, describe the policies and programs that the government promises to follow to be eligible for debt relief. In an effort to recognize the sovereignty of debtor nations, the IMF and World Bank have adapted Structural Adjustment Programme requirements so that nations seeking debt relief must develop their own economic plans, or PRSPs, to promote economic growth and reduce poverty.

Former World Bank economist William Easterly criticizes the PRSP process in his book *The White Man's Burden: Why The West's Efforts to Aid the Rest Have Done So Much Ill and So Little Good*. He believes use of PRSPs simply continues IMF and World Bank policies of overriding the sovereignty of African nations. Easterly states:

> The IMF and World Bank have allegedly given up on telling governments what to do. So, instead, they want a government to tell them what it will do in order to get a loan. . . . So the poor-country governments, instead of being told what to do, are now trying to guess what the international agencies will approve their doing.

Proponents of debt relief have stated that in cases of so-called odious debt (debt incurred while under the rule of a corrupt government), creditors should not expect to be repaid, because they knowingly lent money to corrupt leaders. Because lenders knew that their loans would be misspent, misappropriated, or used to repress others, such debts should be cancelled. Examples of odious debts include loans made to the apartheid government of South Africa or to the dictator Mobutu in the Democratic Republic of the Congo.

Nigeria is another example in which externally supported military dictatorships incurred massive public debts. Nigeria owed approximately $30 billion, accumulated in part because the government fell behind in payments and accumulated penalty interest. After the country transitioned to a democracy in 1999, with the election of Olusegun Obasanjo as president, it continued to attempt to repay its debts. Eventually, the Nigerian government successfully argued that it should not have to repay its odious debt. A deal was made in which Nigeria would repay roughly $12 billion in missed payments to its creditors. Through debt cancellation of $18 billion and with proceeds from the nation's lucrative oil industry, Nigeria was able to pay off $30 billion in debt in April 2006.

Nigerian president Olusegun Obasanjo meets with World Bank president Paul Wolfowitz at the World Economic Forum held in Davos, Switzerland, in 2006. Obasanjo encouraged donors to write off Nigeria's debt by driving an anti-corruption campaign within his government. "The legislature cannot wallow in corruption and expect the outside world to take our pleas for debt relief very seriously," he told BBC News in May 2005.

Numerous movements to have Africa's debt cancelled arose during the late 1990s and early 2000s. One special interest group, Jubilee 2000, lobbied wealthy countries to provide debt relief for developing countries around the world and by the end of 2000 had helped bring about international debt forgiveness for 24 countries. Offshoots of the organization include the UK-based Jubilee Debt Campaign and Jubilee USA.

SOURCES OF DEVELOPMENTAL AID

Like debt forgiveness, development assistance promotes economic development. Defined as grants or loans made with the intent to help long-term economic progress, social stability, and/or political development, developmental aid may come as private donations—from international foundations, businesses, nongovernmental organizations, or religious organizations. In addition, money sent home by foreign workers, or remittances, can also support economic development in poor nations. It has been estimated that worldwide private contributions for developmental aid are as high as $34 billion per year.

Since the 1990s NGOs have become increasingly important in implementing developmental aid programs, as Richard H. Robbins explains in his book *Global Problems and the Culture of Capitalism*. The end of the Cold War has made it easier for NGOs to operate without being forced to take sides. Technological advances in communications advances, especially the Internet, have helped create new global communities and bonds between like-minded people across state boundaries. The media's ability to inform more people about global problems has

In December 2000 demonstrators in London, England, call for the cancellation of third world debt during a Jubilee 2000 march.

led to increased awareness and as a result put pressure on governments to solve them.

According the World Bank website, from 1970 to 1985 the amount of developmental aid distributed through international NGOs increased tenfold. More than $7.6 billion in aid to developing countries was spent through NGOs, and today NGOs channel more than 15 percent of developmental aid to poor countries.

OFFICIAL DEVELOPMENT ASSISTANCE (ODA)

Some of the money that NGOs use for developmental aid programs comes from the public sector (that is, from federal, state, or local governments). Developmental aid that comes from governments and that is specifically aimed at helping poor nations improve their economy—and thus reduce poverty—is called Official Development Assistance (ODA).

ODA funding is monitored by the Organization for Economic Cooperation and Development (OECD), an international organization of 30 economically advanced democratic countries that works to improve the economic and social welfare of developing countries. Like the World Bank and IMF, the OECD originated in the 1940s, with the purpose of advancing the reconstruction of Europe after World War II. Within the OECD, a specialized committee of wealthy countries known as the Development Assistance Committee (DAC) coordinates assistance policies and monitors the flow of aid to developing countries.

Official development assistance may include bilateral grants and loans, technology assistance, food aid, subsidies, emergency and distress relief, and debt forgiveness. ODA can also consist of multilateral grants made to UN agencies and to other international organizations serving developing countries. ODA's purpose is long-term economic and social development of developing countries, rather than short-term assistance in response to disasters.

GOAL OF 0.7 PERCENT

Through UN General Assembly Resolution 2626, the 22 member nations of DAC have agreed to increase the amount of ODA they give annually so that it equals 0.7 percent of their gross national income (GNI). For the past two decades annual ODA has averaged around $50 to $60 billion per year, although during the 1990s it declined significantly. However, beginning in the 2000s ODA amounts increased, reaching more than $100 billion in 2005. A large factor for recent aid increases in ODA has been the "war on terrorism," especially for the United States, the largest donor in dollar terms. As a result, greater amounts of aid have been allocated for helping stabilize regions viewed as security threats to the developed world.

Figure 1 (on page 52) shows the Official Development Assistance given in 2005 by individual DAC members. The combined amount totals almost $106.5 billion. That figure represents 0.33 percent of DAC members' combined GNI, which is an increase from 2004, when only 0.26 percent of DAC member's GNI went to ODA.

As the graph indicates, the United States is the world's largest contributor of ODA in actual dollars, giving approximately $27.5 billion in 2005, which was an increase of about 38 percent from the $19.7 billion given in 2004. However in terms of GNI, the United States is one of the smallest contributors of the DAC countries. In 2005 U.S. ODA was only 0.22 percent of the U.S. gross national income, far short of the UN target goal of 0.7 percent.

The amount of foreign aid given by the United States had been declining since the mid-1980s, and only since 2001 has it started increasing. Most of this ODA increase can be attributed to debt relief, reconstruction aid in Iraq ($3.5 billion), reconstruction and anti-narcotics programs in Afghanistan (1.5 billion), and aid to sub-Saharan Africa ($4.1 billion).

FIGURE 1
NET OFFICIAL DEVELOPMENT ASSISTANCE (ODA) IN 2005

Net ODA in 2005 - Amounts

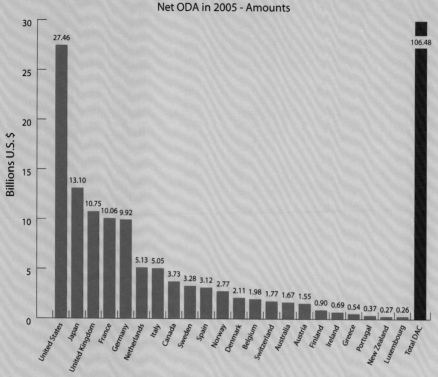

Net ODA in 2005 - As a Percentage of GNI

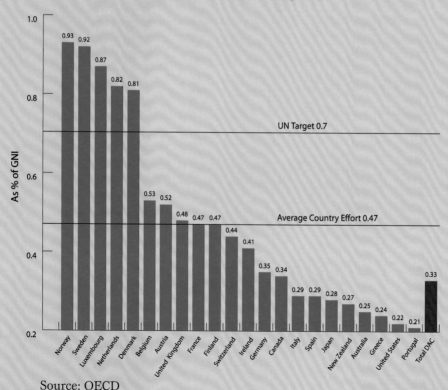

Source: OECD

The largest donor countries in terms of dollar amounts in 2005 were, in descending order, the United States, Japan, the United Kingdom, France, and Germany. However, in terms of the 0.7 percent GNI target, only 5 of the 22 countries from the DAC have matched or exceeded their commitment: Norway, Sweden, Luxembourg, the Netherlands, and Denmark.

WHERE DOES ODA GO?

Unfortunately, Official Development Assistance does not always go to the least developed countries. In 2004, the top ten recipients of ODA were Iraq, the Democratic Republic of the Congo, China, India, Indonesia, Afghanistan, Egypt, Pakistan, Ghana, and Vietnam. (Of all of these countries, only the Democratic Republic of the Congo is identified as a least developed country, and its inclusion on the list reflects a massive infusion of debt relief.)

In recent years, sub-Saharan African countries have not typically received much aid. Figure 2 illustrates the amount of total ODA that has gone to Africa since 1990, in comparison with total amount of ODA given worldwide. The spike in aid showing for 2005 and 2006 reflects major debt relief granted to Iraq and Nigeria (a total of $19 billion in 2005 and $11 billion in 2006). At the rate that ODA is being increased by DAC countries, the OECD estimates that by 2010 Official Development Assistance will amount to only 0.36 percent of combined DAC gross national incomes—far short of the UN target of 0.7 percent.

In 2004, when total ODA was $79.5 billion, the least developed countries received about only 22 percent of official development aid. Figure 3 shows that the top 10 least developed country recipients of ODA were the Democratic Republic of the Congo, Afghanistan, Tanzania, Ethiopia, Mozambique, Bangladesh, Uganda, Zambia, Madagascar, and Angola.

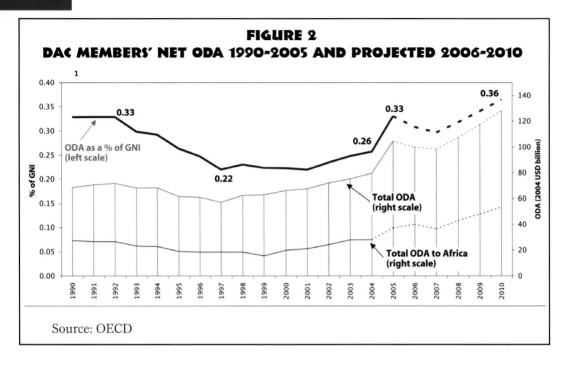

FIGURE 2
DAC MEMBERS' NET ODA 1990-2005 AND PROJECTED 2006-2010

Source: OECD

SHORTFALL IN ODA COMMITMENTS

As the economies of the DAC countries have grown, their dollar amounts of aid donations have also grown. However, especially since 1992, the shortfall—the difference between total ODA disbursed versus the promised 0.7 percent of GNI—has grown. The amount of shortfall that would have accumulated since 1970—if DAC countries had fulfilled their commitment from the very start—is more than $2.5 trillion. This amount of assistance could have made a significant impact on the economic development of the world's poorest countries—Africa in particular.

DEVELOPMENTAL AID AND THE UN MILLENNIUM DEVELOPMENT GOALS

After being passed in 2000, the UN Millennium Development Goals have helped target aid to the goal of poverty reduction. For

LEAST DEVELOPED COUNTRIES (LDCS) IN AFRICA

UN designation of countries as LDCs is based on criteria of low income (per capita GDP under $750), weak human resources (based on indicators such as nutrition, health, education, and adult literacy), and economic vulnerability (based on indicators such as stability of agricultural production and of export market). As of 2005, 34 countries in Africa were identified as LDCs:

Angola	Liberia
Benin	Madagascar
Burkina Faso	Malawi
Burundi	Mali
Cape Verde	Mauritania
Central African Republic	Mozambique
Chad	Niger
Comoros	Rwanda
Democratic Republic of the Congo	Sao Tome & Principe
Djibouti	Senegal
Equatorial Guinea	Sierra Leone
Eritrea	Somalia
Ethiopia	Sudan
Gambia	Tanzania
Guinea	Togo
Guinea-Bissau	Uganda
Lesotho	Zambia

Source: http://www.un.org/special-rep/ohrlls/ldc/list.htm, accessed 2006.

example, at the 2002 G8 summit, U.S. president George W. Bush announced the establishment of the Millennium Challenge Account initiative, which directs conditional foreign aid to low- and low-middle income countries identified as having sound economic policies (based on free market economic reforms) and good governance. Among the countries considered eligible were Ghana, Benin, Senegal, Mozambique, Lesotho, Madagascar, Mali, and Morocco. The foreign aid agency created to administer the initiative, the Millennium Challenge Corporation, was established in

At the G8 summit held July 8, 2005, in Gleneagles, Scotland, African leaders pose with the heads of the eight most industrialized nations. At that time, G8 leaders pledged $25 billion in aid to sub-Saharan Africa.

2004, with a proposed budget of $1.7 billion in 2004, $3.3 billion in 2005, and $5 billion each year after that.

In July 2005 government leaders at the G8 summit held in Gleneagles, Scotland, announced they would write off $40 billion in debt to the poorest nations and double aid to Africa. The group pledged $50 billion in additional aid that would begin flowing five years later, in 2010, with half of the increase going to Africa. (In 2005 overall aid to poor nations was estimated at $80 billion a year.)

In 2006 Oxfam criticized G8 leaders for not fulfilling the promises made at the Gleneagles meeting, when they committed to doubling aid to Africa. The charity organization observed that debt write-off should not be included in promised developmental aid figures, and noted that most of the $21 billion increase in spending from 2004 to 2005 reflected debt cancellation affecting Nigeria and Iraq.

The OECD is hopeful that as the date approaches for proposed fulfillment of the Millennium Development Goals—by the year 2015—there will be greater incentive for donor countries to increase their aid. In April 2004 the Minister of Finance and

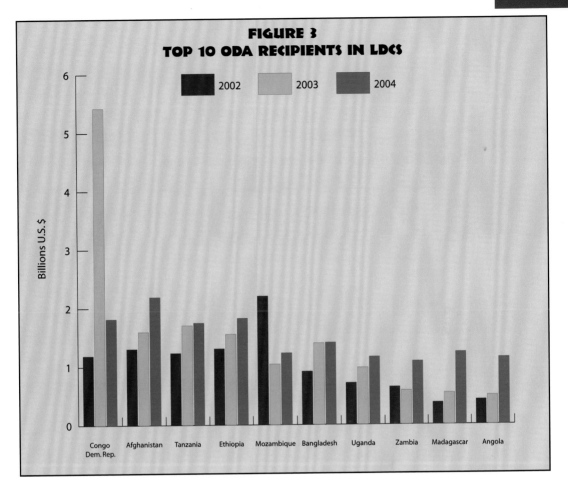

FIGURE 3
TOP 10 ODA RECIPIENTS IN LDCS

National Economy for Sudan, Elzubier Ahmed Elhassan, noted that "the most significant obstacles to achieving the MDGs, Millennium Development Goals, is the shortfall—that is, the difference between what developing countries promised in ODA over the years and what they delivered."

Before the Gleneagles announcement, many European countries reiterated their commitment to meet by 2015 the UN target of giving 0.7 percent of their gross national income to developing countries. The European nations announced that by 2010 their ODA would reflect an interim target of 0.56 percent of GNI. However, many nations remain concerned about the potential negative effect of aid spending on their economies and pressures on public budgets.

IMPROVING ACCESS TO WORLD TRADE

The international community has the power to help Africa develop economically through world trade, especially since the continent currently has minimal participation in the global economy. According to Oxfam, if Africa could increase its share in world trade by just 1 percent, that amount would provide a monetary windfall of $70 billion—which is far greater than the amount the continent receives through aid and debt relief combined.

ECONOMIC GLOBALIZATION

The eighth Millennium Goal calls upon world nations to develop a global partnership for development by increasing aid, relieving debt, and giving poor countries fair access to global markets. Some critics blame Africa's economic troubles on world trade practices that do not allow fair access to world markets. Current policies have discouraged industrial development and lowered prices for many of Africa's commodity exports.

Economic globalization (the worldwide interdependence among countries selling their goods and services) has had a negative impact on the very poor, claims former South African president Nelson Mandela. In the 2002 executive summary of *Oil and Gas Report*, published by the UN Environment Program's Department of Technology, he stated, "We welcome the process of globalization. It is inescapable and irreversible." But he also warned:

> [I]f globalization is to create real peace and stability across the world, it must be a process benefiting all. It must not allow the most economically and politically powerful countries to dominate and submerge the countries of the weaker and peripheral regions. It should not be allowed to drain the wealth of smaller countries towards the larger ones, or to increase inequality between richer and poorer regions.

UNFAIR SUBSIDIES

A major complaint about world trade is the negative effect that agricultural policies of rich countries have on poor nations. Many U.S. and European Union (EU) countries heavily subsidize their farmers. The practice distorts market realities—artificially making rich countries' products cheaper so they can be sold at much lower prices than the goods produced in developing countries can. Poor African nations cannot afford to subsidize their farmers. They are left to struggle to sell their commodities of cotton, beef, tomatoes, or coffee in markets where U.S. and EU governments have provided significant agricultural subsidies to their citizens.

For example, the United States subsidizes its 25,000 cotton farmers with $4 billion per year, which allows them to export the crop at one-third of what it costs to produce. As a result, some economists estimate, the world price for cotton is 25 percent lower than it would be without such subsidies. Because of the inequity of subsidized agricultural commodities, says the charity group

In Ukunda, Kenya, the site of a World Trade Organization meeting in 2005, a demonstrator carries a poster accusing the WTO of fostering unfair trade practices. The WTO is a global organization that establishes rules of free trade among most of the world's nations through treaties and agreements.

Christian Aid, reforms such as trade liberalization do not promote economic development in low-income nations.

The EU Common Agricultural Policy, the U.S. Farm Bill, and programs of other rich nations provide some $350 billion per year in subsidies to their agricultural industries. That equals more than the total annual amount of ODA. Such subsidies allow farmers of rich countries to export their surplus crops within the world market at low prices, often as food aid. However, critics refer to the practice as "food dumping."

The Commission for Africa, an organization launched by British prime minister Tony Blair in 2004 to provide guidance to African countries and world leaders, has addressed the effect of unfair trade policies on Africa. In their report, *Our Common Interest*, published in March 2005, commission members, most of whom were Africans, described the disparity in global trade:

We live in a world where rich nations spend as much as the entire income of all the people in Africa subsidizing the unnecessary production of unwanted food—to the tune of almost US$1 billion a day. While in Africa hunger is a key factor in more deaths than all the continent's infectious diseases put together.

We live in a world where every cow in Europe has received almost US$2 a day in subsidies—double, grotesquely, the average income in Africa. And Japanese cows nearly US$4.

… the agricultural sectors of many G8 and EU countries are the most heavily subsidized and protected in the economies of the industrialized world. Rich countries spend around US$350 billion a year on agricultural protection and subsidies – which is 16 times their aid to Africa. The European Union is responsible for 35 percent of this, the United States for 27 percent and Japan for 22 percent.

Since 1990, the prices for many of Africa's exports have been cut in half, and the economies of developing nations have had to absorb the losses. The impact of dumping any subsidized products on developing nations is serious: it hinders local markets, and in the case of agriculture, can make farmers go out of business, leaving communities vulnerable to poverty and hunger.

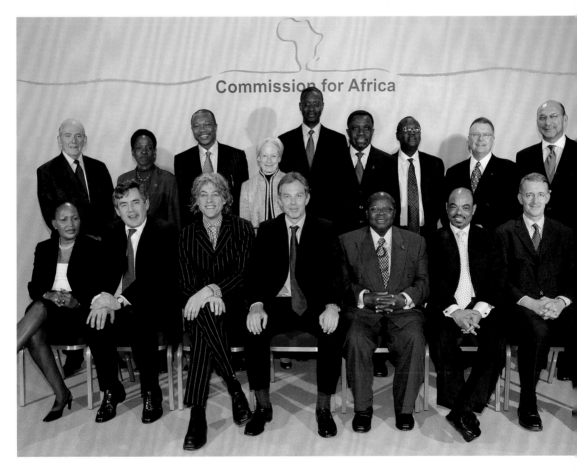

British prime minister Tony Blair (front, center) poses with members of the Commission for Africa, an organization he established in 2004 to propose solutions for problems such as AIDS/HIV, conflict, and poverty in the continent.

TARIFFS AND TRADE BARRIERS

In addition, many wealthy nations charge high tariffs (or taxes) on agricultural and textile industry imports—goods that are frequently produced by developing countries. Rich countries sometimes maintain trade barriers on such items, essentially preventing their importation. As a result, the export market of African nations and other developing countries is reduced, as is their ability to participate in world trade.

Trade liberalization policies of the Structural Adjustment Programme required that participating nations open up their markets to the rest of the world, but poor countries had to contend with the subsidies and trade barriers of wealthy nations. As a result, developing countries have not been able to compete. Oxfam reports that "[t]he 48 least-developed countries (LDCs), home to 10 per cent of the world's citizens, have seen their share of world exports decline to a tiny 0.4 [percent] over the past two decades." At the same time, the NGO notes, the European Union and the United States have accounted for almost 50 percent of world exports.

Tariffs on goods exported from Africa have also discouraged investment in manufacturing in African countries. Because of import duties imposed on manufactured products exported from developing countries, international corporations find that it is cheaper to export raw materials for processing in industrialized countries than to process a product in Africa. Under current conditions, trade liberalization has undermined Africa's ability to develop manufacturing, says the charity group Christian Aid. And growth in that sector is important, Christian Aid notes: "It is the development of manufacturing that Africa needs if it is ever to trade its way out of poverty."

The World Trade Organization (WTO), an international group that facilitates global trade, has been widely criticized for doing little to help developing nations overcome poverty. Critics

complain that the global trading system rules established by the
WTO, which consists of 149 member states, favor the richer,
more powerful countries and global corporations. These countries and businesses wield more influence when determining the
conditions of world trade. Meanwhile, developing countries and
organizations representing them have been excluded from negotiations and had their recommendations ignored.

In response, WTO officials note that many low-income countries often receive preferential treatment with some products
and that these nations are exempt from certain regulations that
have been imposed on wealthier ones. However, the WTO has
been unable to make the global trade system more equitable for
developing countries by eliminating the subsidy programs or
reducing the trade barriers of wealthier nations.

In 2001 the members of the World Trade Organization began
what became a series of negotiations on how to change the global

**Negotiations among members of the World Trade Organization to lower trade barriers for developing
nations began in November 2001 in Doha, Qatar. Subsequent discussions, referred to as the Doha round
of global trade talks, failed to bring about an agreement.**

trade system so that farmers of developing countries would have better access. These talks included calls for eliminating export subsidies and reducing domestic subsidies of wealthy nations. Because the first set of negotiations took place in Doha, Qatar, they were subsequently referred to as the Doha development round of WTO negotiations.

However, despite several follow-up meetings, as of mid-2006 the Doha rounds had not produced an accord. Many wealthy countries remained reluctant to remove subsidies because of domestic political concerns.

FAIR TRADE CAMPAIGN

Some NGOs recognize that world trade can be a powerful force to support economic growth and thus reduce poverty in many developing countries around the world. Some antipoverty groups

The British charity organization Oxfam launched a global trade awareness campaign in 2002 in Hong Kong, China. In a symbolic gesture condemning WTO practices, a shipping container labeled "Make Trade Fair" crushes a second container that has been decorated with various trade rules.

have sought to work for changes in the rules of international trade by promoting a "Make Trade Fair" campaign.

This international movement seeks to help farmers in developing countries receive guaranteed, fair prices for their goods, not the artificially lowered prices offered on the global market. Products such as tea, coffee, bananas, and sugar that are purchased according to this fair price policy carry a "Fairtrade" or "Fair trade certified" label. Supermarkets and specialty stores in many rich countries now stock fair trade goods (including food items, clothing, and flowers), which consumers can buy to support poor communities.

In addition to helping farmers in developing countries gain access to international markets, Fair Trade organizations also work to help them develop the knowledge and skills to improve and grow their businesses. Fair trade groups are based in 15 European countries, as well as Australia, New Zealand, Canada, Japan, Mexico, and the United States.

TRADE WITH CHINA AND INDIA

Economic growth in the Asian countries of China and India over the past two decades has affected Africa, as the two countries have become trading partners with many African nations. In recent years China has intensified its activities in Africa—making numerous trade agreements, investing in infrastructure, and extracting energy.

Between 2000 and 2005, sub-Sahara's economic growth rate almost doubled, from 3 percent to approximately 5.8 percent, in large part because of increased trade with China. In fact, during that five-year period China's overall trade with Africa rose from $10.6 billion to $40 billion, and it continues to increase. However, much of China's investment in Africa has focused on extracting its natural resources, particularly oil, copper, platinum, and timber. As demand for these commodities has

Copper mining operations at the Ruashi mine near the city of Lubumbashi, in the Democratic Republic of the Congo. The country is among several in sub-Saharan Africa benefiting economically from exporting its natural resources to China.

increased, their prices have surged, which has benefited the African economy. Some critics complain that the Chinese seem to be following the pattern established by Europeans in colonial times: treating Africa as a source of raw materials and a market for processed goods.

Some Western governments are troubled by China's development of increasingly close ties with African governments considered corrupt and neglectful of human rights and democratic values. Of particular concern are the governments of Angola, Nigeria, Sudan, and Zimbabwe. Chinese leaders have stated that they have no intention of interfering with the internal affairs of these African nations.

DEALING WITH HEALTH ISSUES

I n December 1948 the United Nations adopted the Universal Declaration of Human Rights. It asserts, "Everyone has the right to a standard of living adequate for the health and well-being of himself and of his family, including food, clothing, housing and medical care." However, since the 1980s many of the citizens of African nations have found these benefits and rights eluding them.

Adequate health care has declined in Africa, as evidenced by the dramatic decrease in average lifespan. In the 1960s and 1970s, the average African could expect to live to the age of 62. However, since then average life expectancy has plummeted, particularly in sub-Saharan Africa, where today it is 47 years or less. Much of this decrease in life expectancy is due to infectious diseases.

INFECTIOUS DISEASES

In 2002, of the almost 11 million people who died of infectious diseases worldwide, almost 6

Unwillingness by the South African government to acknowledge the need for funding treatment of HIV/AIDS led activists in Cape Town to protest in 2004.

million were from sub-Saharan Africa. As poverty has advanced on the continent and the standard of living has fallen, more and more people have become vulnerable to infectious diseases such as AIDS, malaria, and tuberculosis (TB).

The greatest killer has been HIV/AIDS. Since the early 1980s, AIDS has killed more than 28 million people around the world. Approximately 26 million of those deaths have occurred in sub-Saharan Africa, where HIV/AIDS is ravaging the region. UNAIDS, a United Nations program comprised of 10 UN agencies working together to fight HIV/AIDS, compiles yearly statistics on its global impact. In 2005, UNAIDS reported, there were 40 million people living with HIV (25.8 million of them in sub-Saharan Africa), 4.9 million new HIV infections (3.2 million in sub-Saharan Africa), and 3.1 million AIDS deaths (2.4 million in

Africa). The southernmost countries of Africa have suffered the most from the deadly disease. The UN has reported that the life expectancy in nine southern African countries (Botswana, Central African Republic, Lesotho, Malawi, Mozambique, Rwanda, Swaziland, Zambia and Zimbabwe) has fallen to less than 40 years.

The second deadliest disease of sub-Saharan Africa is malaria, which is carried by mosquitoes. Almost 90 percent of the world's malaria deaths occur in this region, and the disease is the leading cause of death for children—killing up to 3 million each year. More than 3,000 children in Africa die from malaria every day. Other illnesses that have also been devastating to Africa's children are diarrheal diseases and acute respiratory infections, including pneumonia.

Tuberculosis is Africa's third greatest killer. Its rise in sub-Saharan Africa is attributed to the increase of HIV/AIDS, which

Malaria continues to rage across sub-Saharan Africa despite the efforts of many governments to educate their citizens about how to prevent infection from mosquitoes, which carry the disease. A poster in Zambia promotes the use of insecticide-treated bed nets to prevent mosquito bites. In Uganda, a health worker hands out treated nets.

depresses the body's immune system so that it cannot fight infection by the tuberculosis bacteria. The number of TB cases has risen five-fold in sub-Saharan Africa since the 1980s, and the region now accounts for more than 25 percent of tuberculosis cases in the world. The World Health Organization reports that as a proportion of population, there are more deaths and incidents of tuberculosis (TB) in Africa than anywhere else, with 587,000 deaths in 2004 alone—just under one third of the world's total.

Some diseases are now the cause of poverty. AIDS, malaria, and tuberculosis impact economic growth, as epidemics reduce work productivity and decimate the workforce. The pain and suffering caused to sufferers and families—especially when a sole income provider falls ill—adds to the wide human and economic loss. For children, schooling and social development can often be hindered, while investors may hesitate to invest in countries where diseases are prevalent. In southern African countries AIDS may soon cause massive food shortages: it is estimated that by 2020 one fifth of the agricultural workers in the region will have died from the disease.

LACK OF FOOD, WATER, AND PROPER SANITATION

The spread of disease in Africa has been rapid because of the lack of essentials taken for granted in industrialized nations. For many decades, food shortages have occurred because of droughts, famines, and conflicts. CARE, a humanitarian organization that fights global poverty, reported in 2005 that 25 African countries were in a state of food emergency. The international agency noted that hunger was afflicting an estimated 10 million in Southern Africa (Zimbabwe, Malawi, Zambia, Lesotho, Mozambique), 5 million in West Africa (Niger, Chad, and Mali), and 23 million in East Africa (Ethiopia, Sudan, and Somalia). The lack of food has caused widespread malnutrition,

Lack of nutrition has made many African children susceptible to disease. In Butsiri, in the Democratic Republic of the Congo, a malnourished boy is weighed at a rural nutrition center run in conjunction with Médecins sans Frontières (Doctors Without Borders).

which can lead to death—approximately 4.5 million children under the age of 5 die of malnutrition each year in sub-Saharan Africa. Malnutrition also weakens the body, making it vulnerable to deadly diseases.

Similarly, the lack of clean water and sanitation in many African countries allows contaminated water to introduce diseases that kill. WHO reports that nearly 1.2 billion people around the world do not have safe drinking water and another 2.6 billion live without basic sanitation. In sub-Saharan Africa the lack of clean water and sanitation has led to the deaths of millions of children and adults from cholera, dysentery, and other diseases associated with water-borne pathogens.

LIMITED ACCESS TO HEALTH CARE

Both malaria and tuberculosis have been controlled and even eliminated in industrialized parts of the world. However, WHO and other health organizations repeatedly point out that many problems in Africa and elsewhere stem from "diseases of poverty": people in developing countries are too poor to afford decent health care and life-saving medicine. Almost half of all people in sub-Saharan Africa—some 300 million—lack access to health care services and modern medicines.

Africa's health care systems began to suffer in the 1980s, when many poor nations began making extensive cuts in their national budgets so they could repay massive debts. Governments looking for additional loans had to meet Structural Adjustment Programme conditions, which called for significant cuts in public

At a feeding center in Malange, Angola, the nongovernmental organization Médecins sans Frontières provides food to refugees from civil war.

welfare spending. These cuts often hit the health and education sectors the hardest. At the very beginning of the AIDS epidemic, many African governments had little or no funding to provide the health care services and preventative education programs needed to fight it. Without adequate public health programs, AIDS and other infectious diseases quickly spread, claiming millions of lives. Limited public health budgets also meant there was no money for training medical workers and volunteers, providing immunization programs, or building medical facilities.

In an article posted on the Africa Action website, Ann-Louise Colgan states that public health care systems would have been better than private ones in addressing health issues in Africa:

> When infectious diseases constitute the greatest challenge to health in Africa, public health services are essential. Private health care cannot make the necessary interventions at the community level, . . . is less effective at prevention, and is less able to cope with epidemic situations. Successfully responding to the spread of HIV/AIDS and other diseases in Africa requires strong public health care services.

As health care in Africa was transformed from a public service to a privatized system, patients had to pay user fees in order to receive treatment. However, people living in poverty could not afford to pay for medical care when they became ill. The institution of user fees in privatized health systems has resulted in hundreds of thousand of deaths, concludes Chris James, of the NGO Save the Children UK. In an October 2005 report in the *British Medical Journal*, the author stated that eliminating the practice of user fees in 20 African countries could prevent the deaths of 153,000 to 305,000 children under the age of 5 each year.

When developmental aid is given to fund medical training and abolish user fees, the result is improved access to health care for many impoverished Africans. This was the case in Uganda, where from 2000 to 2005 the United Kingdom's Department for International Development gave financial support amounting to about $600 million. That funding allowed the government to abolish health user fees, recruit 3,000 trained health workers, and more than double immunization rates for children under five, from 41 percent to 83 percent.

FIGHTING DISEASE IN AFRICA

Because malnutrition and the lack of clean water foster the spread of illnesses, health-oriented foreign aid has focused not only on providing treatment for the afflicted but also on developing prevention programs and reducing poverty. Among the United Nations agencies providing aid are UNICEF, which promotes children's health; the World Health Organization, which works in public health and disease control; and the World Food Program, which helps feed Africans who have become refugees or been displaced within their own country by drought, famine or warfare. UNICEF, WHO, and WFP are also represented in the

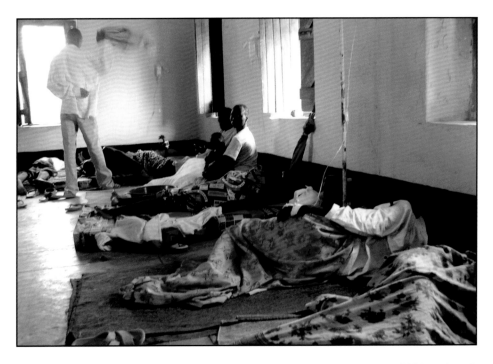

Doctors from UNICEF struggle to stop an outbreak of cholera in February 2006 in the village of Yei, in southern Sudan.

joint UN program UNAIDS, which was established in 1996 to fight the HIV/AIDS pandemic.

Other nongovernmental organizations, such as the International Committee of the Red Cross (ICRC), Médecins Sans Frontières (MSF, also called Doctors Without Borders), and Oxfam provide valuable humanitarian health assistance in emergency situations. Many of these NGOs also battle disease and malnutrition in Africa by working in a range of long-term educational, health, and community development projects. For example, the ICRC trains local and volunteer doctors, nurses, and assistants to diagnose and treat patients; helps deliver medications and medical equipment; and establishes nutritional programs.

Drinking water supply and sanitation projects such as USAID's Water for the Poor Initiative and various other partnerships have supported the development of infrastructures to bring water and sanitation to people in Africa. In some cases both government and private resources work together as is the case with the West Africa Water Initiative, which brings water and sanitation to communities in the countries of Ghana, Mali, and Niger. Initiatives that improve access to water sources also reduce the likelihood of food shortages when the infrastructure provides irrigation systems that farmers can use.

GLOBAL HEALTH INITIATIVES

Public institutions have partnered with the private sector to make additional resources available to fight deadly diseases. Many of these global health initiatives are massive networks comprised of international organizations, countries, governmental and nongovernmental organizations, and donors from the private and public sectors. Several of these global initiatives strive to accomplish the UN Millennium Development Goals of reducing child mortality, improving maternal health, and combating AIDS/HIV, malaria, and other diseases.

Some of these health initiatives focus on a single disease. The Global Partnership to Stop TB seeks to eliminate tuberculosis around the world by providing prevention measures; effective treatment; and support for development of new diagnostic tests, drugs, and vaccines. More than 90 organizations are involved in the Roll Back Malaria campaign, which aims to cut the worldwide malaria mortality rate in half by 2010.

However, a lack of funding has reduced the effectiveness of some global health initiatives. Despite the efforts of the Roll Back Malaria campaign, the number of malaria cases worldwide has increased since the health initiative's founding in 1998. Its administrators estimate that $3.2 billion a year is needed for the campaign to support malaria prevention strategies, but far less is donated each year.

On the other hand, the Global Polio Eradication Initiative, launched in 1988, has been able to successfully immunize hundreds of thousands of children in 125 countries against the paralyzing disease. The campaign required development of systems such as cold boxes, used to store polio vaccines and keep them effective while being transported to remote villages. In Africa, extensive polio vaccination efforts have been made in Djibouti, Eritrea, Ethiopia, Somalia, Sudan, Yemen, Kenya, and the Democratic Republic of the Congo.

GLOBAL ALLIANCE FOR VACCINES AND IMMUNIZATION

One global health initiative works to defeat several vaccine-preventable diseases that seldom occur in industrialized countries. Although there are vaccines for *Haemophilus influenzae* type b (Hib) and yellow fever, these diseases continue to kill millions of children in the poorest regions of the world, where there is little access to immunization. Established in 1999, the Global Alliance for Vaccines and Immunization (GAVI) is a coalition

Efforts to vaccinate children in developing countries through the Global Polio Eradication Initiative have cost more than $3 billion and drawn upon the resources of more than 20 million volunteers. Here a worker helps with the vaccination of a child in the village of Garin Bajini, in Niger, in 2003.

among governments, UN agencies (such as UNICEF and WHO), charitable foundations, vaccine manufacturers, and scientists—working together to defeat vaccine-preventable diseases and develop new ways to prevent and treat other diseases. GAVI is funding research and development in the making of new vaccines for meningococcal disease, pneumococcal disease, and rotavirus diarrhea.

In 2004 GAVI announced that 41.6 million children around the world had been vaccinated against hepatitis B, 5.6 million against Hib, 3.2 million against yellow fever, and 9.6 million with other basic vaccines. The organization's goal is to have 90 percent of the world's poorest children vaccinated by 2015. It has already reported that it has reversed the decline in vaccination rates in many African countries.

The Global Alliance for Vaccines and Immunization has received significant funding from the Bill & Melinda Gates

Foundation, which provided the bulk of GAVI's funding when the initiative was founded. In 1999, the Gates Foundation donated $750 million to GAVI for use over a five-year period; in 2005 the Gates Foundation bestowed another $750 million on the organization for use over the next ten years.

GLOBAL FUND TO FIGHT AIDS, TUBERCULOSIS AND MALARIA

Another major initiative is the Geneva-based Global Fund to Fight AIDS, Tuberculosis and Malaria (often called "the Fund" for short), which was officially launched in 2002 to combat these three diseases of poverty. The Fund collaborates with other groups, including UNAIDS, the World Health Organization, the United Nations Development Program, and government donors.

Bill and Melinda Gates hold two African children during a visit to the Manhica Health Research Center in Mozambique. The center received a $168 million grant from the Bill & Melinda Gates Foundation for use in malaria research.

Some major donor countries are the United States, Great Britain, and France.

Rather than tackling specific issues as a development agency, the Fund serves as a funding mechanism, by providing grants for various health programs that are initiated and developed by local communities or national governments. With HIV/AIDS, for example, the Fund has fostered large-scale prevention programs and the expansion of testing and counseling initiatives. Worldwide, programs and services financed by the Fund have provided antiretroviral treatment for AIDS to 220,000 people, treated 600,000 for tuberculosis, and distributed malaria-prevention bed nets to 3.1 million. As of December 2005, the Fund had approved grants to 128 countries, committing approximately $4.4 billion (with approximately 60 percent of that funding earmarked for Africa).

However, the Fund has suffered from poor funding, slow distribution, and political obstacles. Budget limitations were alleviated somewhat in August 2006, when the organization received a $500 million donation, to be given over the course of five years, from the Bill & Melinda Gates Foundation. Despite the donation, the Global Fund reported its budget was still short another $1.5 billion for 2006.

NATIONAL GOVERNMENT LEADERSHIP

The response of African governments to health issues in their own countries has varied. In the more industrialized nation of South Africa, which is relatively wealthy, President Thabo Mbeki refused to acknowledge a connection between AIDS and HIV. As a result, for many years he did not allow his government to sponsor national prevention programs. It was not until March 2003 that public outrage and international pressure finally forced him to fund HIV/AIDS programs for South African citizens.

Other nations, such as Senegal, showed a more proactive response to the AIDS crisis, as officials quickly recognized the severity of the problem. Although the country is among the world's poorest, its government channeled resources into fighting the spread of HIV infection. Senegal health officials used the media to effectively raise awareness and promote prevention strategies, even though talking about sexual practices broke religious and cultural taboos. Once it was determined that universal access to antiretrovirals (the drugs used to treat HIV/AIDS) effectively slowed the spread of the disease, Senegalese agencies worked to increase access to these essential medicines. In a UNAID report published in 1999, the agency explained that Senegal benefited from a strong infrastructure:

In Senegal, a teacher uses posters as he discusses HIV/AIDS prevention. During the 1980s and 1990s the Senegalese government effectively fought the spread of the deadly disease by continuing to provide health education services despite a limited budget.

[T]here was much in the social structure of Senegal as well as in the structure of its health services even before the advent of AIDS that favored a response once the threat of an HIV epidemic became clear. But it was the determined use of those existing advantages to generate a national response early on that can be credited with the fact that, at the end of the 1990s, Senegal has one of the lowest rates of HIV infection in sub-Saharan Africa.

Similarly, Uganda's government showed leadership, taking steps in the 1980s to stop the spread of AIDS by educating its people about the disease, with apparent success. For example, HIV prevalence among pregnant women (one statistical method used to measure the disease) dropped in Uganda from 30 percent in the 1980s to 6.5 percent in the early 2000s.

Many nations have recognized that the imposition of user fees has prevented its impoverished people from receiving health services. As a result, the governments of Botswana, Ethiopia, Tanzania, Senegal, and Zambia have tried to provide free HIV treatment for patients, usually with the help of funding from government resources and donor contributions.

MAKING ANTIRETROVIRAL DRUGS AFFORDABLE

Developing countries often cannot afford to pay for the expensive brand-name antiretrovirals produced by major pharmaceutical companies, which assert that high prices are necessary to recoup costs of research and development. Pharmaceutical companies hold patents on their brand-name products to ensure control over their manufacture and sale. Such products are also protected by WTO patent rules known as Trade-Related Aspects of Intellectual Property, or TRIPS.

Established in 1994, TRIPS grants the manufacturer of a specific product exclusive patent rights to that product for 20 years, including the right to set prices. Activists, NGOs, and developing countries have criticized TRIPS because they apply to pharmaceuticals. The patent rules prevent the governments of poor countries from negotiating drug prices for lifesaving drugs such as antiretrovirals. Antipoverty groups point out that such restrictions run counter to the eighth UN Millennium Goal, which promotes the development of global partnerships in which developing countries have "access to affordable essential drugs."

In 2001, at the WTO summit in Doha, 142 member countries agreed that developing countries could take action to override the patent rights of major pharmaceutical companies. The Doha Declaration on TRIPS and Public Health gave the governments of poor countries the right to ask domestic manufacturers to make generic drugs (lower-priced drugs that are biologically equivalent to patented medications), if those offered by big drug companies were too expensive.

Under certain conditions, WTO patent rules allow "compulsory licensing," in which poor governments can force patent holders to grant use, or license, to their products so they can be manufactured domestically or in a another country The Doha Declaration affirmed the right of developing countries to use compulsory licensing in cases of public health crises. However, most poor countries do not have sophisticated domestic pharmaceutical industries, so they cannot manufacture the generic medicines themselves. And a technicality in WTO rules did not allow countries to legally import cheaper generics made under compulsory licensing by a third country. According to TRIPS, doing so would infringe on the patent rights of the original manufacturer. As a result, developing countries were prohibited from importing generic drugs from other nations, such as Brazil or India, which have generic pharmaceutical industries.

It took two years before WTO member nations could agree to temporarily waive such prohibitions. In August 2003 the organization agreed to legal changes that would allow member countries, such as Brazil and India, to export pharmaceutical products made under compulsory licensing. The agreement allowed eligible WTO members (mainly least developed countries) to import the patented products they required. However, the countries without generic manufacturing capabilities have to ask another government with such capabilities to license a local company to produce and export the needed drug. Oxfam notes that "Few countries, if any, will be prepared to help other countries in this way, as [compulsory licensing] would provoke retaliation by the US, which fiercely defends the commercial interests of the pharmaceutical corporations. Furthermore, the agreement is wrapped in so much red tape that it becomes largely unworkable."

Another way for developing countries to reduce drug-purchasing costs is "parallel importing," in which a nation shops around for the best prices of brand-name drugs in other countries (usually offered at lower prices than the prices found in the country of origin) and then imports them in bulk. Parallel importing allows poorer countries to import brand-name drugs at low cost. Although TRIPS policies do not address the practice, either to outlaw or approve its use, the United States and many major pharmaceutical companies have strongly opposed parallel importing as an abuse of patent rights.

In the past, many developing countries did not have laws that address the concept of ownership of intellectual property and patent laws. However, WTO members had to establish or modify existing patent laws to conform to TRIPS standards by 2005; some least developed country members do not need to meet TRIPS requirements for patent protection until 2016.

The pharmaceutical industry has fought to protect its intellectual property rights in various international settings, including WTO meetings. In 1998 pharmaceutical manufacturers filed suit against the South African government to fight legislation aimed at reducing the cost of AIDS drugs. Public outcry over the pharmaceutical industries' apparent attitude of "profit over people" and "patents before patients" led the companies to unconditionally withdraw their case in 2001. When Cipla Ltd. of Bombay, one of India's leading generics manufacturers, offered a cocktail of antiretroviral drugs for AIDS to Africa at a per-patient cost of $350 a year, compared to the annual brand-name cost of $10,000, the large multinationals responded by cutting prices, although the costs for brand-name drugs remained higher than those for generics.

In *World Development Report 2006* the World Bank criticized the United States for undermining the purpose of TRIPS by pressuring countries in weaker bargaining positions to make bilateral

In January 2006 former U.S. president Bill Clinton announces that pricing agreements between the Clinton Foundation and nine drugmakers would reduce the costs of the antiretroviral drugs efavirenz and abacavir, as well as HIV diagnostic tests, in 50 developing countries. Making HIV/AIDS diagnostic tools and drugs affordable has helped increase their availability in Africa.

agreements on pharmaceutical purchases, rather than allowing WTO rules to set standards that apply for all countries. The World Bank report noted, "Inequitable as TRIPS may be, it still provides an internationally agreed standard subject to intense scrutiny and study, which does make it harder for rich countries to get more favorable deals in bilateral agreements."

EFFECTIVE PARTNERSHIPS

After much public pressure, major pharmaceutical companies have become more responsive to the needs of developing countries. Some drug manufacturers have joined global health initiatives, by investing time, money, expertise, and drug donations in various programs, including the International Aids Vaccine Initiative, the Accelerating Access Initiative, the Roll Back Malaria Global Partnership, the Stop TB Partnership, the Global Polio Eradication Initiative, and the Global Alliance for Vaccines and Immunization.

In addition to making contributions of money and drugs to global health initiatives, brand-name drug manufacturers have released patents on some drugs so that other companies can produce cheaper generic versions. Major drugmakers have also partnered in programs working within individual African countries. For example, the African Comprehensive HIV/AIDS Partnership is a collaborative effort supported by the Botswana government,

Merck & Co., and the Bill & Melinda Gates Foundation that works to prevent HIV/AIDS and care for, treat, and support its victims. In Kampala, Uganda, a new infectious disease institute was built at Makerere University Medical School with the support of the Pfizer Foundation. Operated by the Academic Alliance for AIDS Care and Prevention in Africa, it is the first large-scale HIV/AIDS clinic in Africa for training medical personnel in treatment options.

The book *Millions Saved: Proven Successes in Global Health*, published by the Center for Global Development, reports on several multipartner international efforts that have been effective in reducing or eliminating debilitating diseases in Africa. Many of these public health initiatives involved the combined efforts of African governments, world nations, international NGOs, and pharmaceutical companies working together.

One successful effort is the Onchocerciasis Control Program (OCP), which significantly reduced the incidence of the parasitic disease in central, western, and eastern parts of rural Africa. Donated medicines helped OCP prevent an estimated 18 million children from contracting onchocerciasis, or river blindness. *Millions Saved* also describes several other successful partnerships efforts, including the eradication of guinea worm infection in sub-Saharan Africa and the elimination of measles in southern Africa through extensive vaccination programs.

7 REFUGEE AID AND PEACE-BUILDING

ivil wars, droughts, and famine have wreaked havoc in many African countries, including Burundi, the Democratic Republic of the Congo, Ethiopia, Rwanda, Sierra Leone, Somalia, and Sudan. Forced from their homes, millions of Africans have migrated to refugee camps in search of food and shelter. The United Nations has placed an active role in providing emergency relief for these refugees, providing assistance through its World Food Program and the Office of the United Nations High Commissioner for Refugees.

FOOD AID AND REFUGEE RELIEF

The WFP organizes the funds for and delivery of food to UNHCR large-scale feeding programs for refugees. Emergency food relief is rushed to areas in which flood, drought, or crop failure has caused famine, or warfare and civil conflict has forced people from their homes. Food shortages in Africa occur more because of conflicts rather

(Opposite) Forming a column stretching 12 miles (20 km) long, approximately 55,000 Rwandan Hutu refugees flee in 1995 from civil strife in their country to Tanzania. Most refugees find safety in camps, where local governments and international organizations such as the United Nations High Commission on Refugees (UNHCR) strive to provide food, water, and medical care.

than from natural disasters such as droughts or floods. "A decade ago, two out of three tons of the food aid provided by WFP was used to help people become self-reliant," a 2004 report on the UN website states. "Today, the picture is reversed, with 80 per cent of WFP resources going to victims of man-made disaster."

The UNHCR defines refugees as "persons who are outside their country and cannot return owing to a well-founded fear of persecution because of their race, religion, nationality, political opinion or membership of a particular social group." The primary purpose of UNHCR is to protect the rights and well-being of refugees. This includes the provision of emergency aid in the form of

food, clothing, shelter, and medical care while in refugee camps. UNHCR also assists refugee when they return home or resettle in another country.

As a result of conflicts in Africa, about 15 million people were internally displaced and another 4.5 million became refugees in nearby nations in 2004. Millions of refugees and displaced people (defined as those who have not crossed international borders) are from Sudan, in the Darfur region, where militias have killed thousands of civilians since conflict broke out in 2003. In 2004 alone approximately 730,000 Sudanese fled to across the border to Chad, Uganda, Ethiopia, and Kenya, where they settled into

Internally displaced families near Nyala town, in Sudan's southern Darfur region, receive food aid from the United Nation's World Food Program in January 2005.

refugee camps. As of 2005 a total of 1.8 million have been displaced within the country.

Children who have become refugees also receive help through UNICEF, which supplies emergency relief, health immunizations, and educational programs. Some UNICEF programs help reunite children with parents or other family members. Through immunization campaigns, UNICEF health workers immunize children in refugee camps against illnesses such as yellow fever, cholera, measles, and meningitis—diseases that tend to spread quickly in camps among people already weakened by malnutrition.

UNICEF also brings aid to regions where conflict is under way. It has negotiated agreements between warring factions to set aside "Days of Tranquility." These days of temporary cease-fires allow aid workers to provide humanitarian relief and health workers to safely vaccinate children.

REFUGEE BURDEN

Assisting refugees is more than a humanitarian mission; it can often become a political issue as well. Some African conflicts have lasted for many years, and large influxes of refugee populations have placed significant economic and social burdens on poor countries already struggling to serve their own citizens. Over time, the leaders of host countries may come to resent refugee-centered aid and the growing numbers of refugees in their lands. In many cases host governments have prevented refugees from integrating into their communities by limiting employment opportunities and movement to other parts of the country. As a result, refugees may live for years in abject poverty, segregated in refugee settlements.

It is understood now that even the most well-intentioned humanitarian assistance such as helping refugees cannot be provided without addressing other issues of the host country. In the wake of growing concern over refugees' rights, activists have pressured both donor and recipient governments to bring about positive change for the plight of refugees.

CONFLICT PREVENTION AND PEACEBUILDING AID

Humanitarian aid workers commonly risk their lives bringing food and supplies to civilians caught in the middle of conflicts. When aid is provided in areas with extremely limited resources, opposing groups may fight over it, so that such aid can become the source of conflict. NGOs delivering humanitarian aid in war zones often need to negotiate with warring factions to ensure that food and supplies can be delivered safely to their intended recipients. Often, these aid organizations are also involved in providing developmental aid to war-scarred regions after conflicts have ceased, with the goal to prevent conflict from breaking out again.

Many peacebuilding government groups and nongovernmental organizations run programs and support initiatives that work to restore communities and help strengthen societies once the fighting has ended. One way to build peace is to set up joint projects and activities that involve members of the previously warring factions. Programs may involve repairing or rebuilding war-damaged buildings and infrastructures or developing joint educational programs. By providing opportunities to reestablish trust and reduce prejudice between former enemies, peacebuilders hope to bring post-conflict normalcy back into the lives of former adversaries and restore a sense of civil society to war-torn communities.

Although peacebuilding programs are often carried out by private organizations, the United Nations also works in conflict prevention and resolution. Because poverty is regarded as a cause of conflict, many programs are designed to promote economic growth. For example, the United Nations Development Program (UNDP) works on relief and developmental efforts, often integrating the two.

POST-CONFLICT AID

NGOs and government organizations work in a variety of ways to help Africans after conflicts have ended. Some projects involve destroying and clearing land mines; others provide support to the victims of mines and establish safety awareness programs in regions where mines riddle the landscape. Aid groups may also help organize the disarmament of troops, the demobilization of forces, and the reintegration of combatants back into society.

In post-conflict rebuilding, people within the same communities often have to face each other and come to terms with the horrors of conflict. This is particularly challenging in cases involving child soldiers. In Africa, children as young as 9 or 10 have been forced—even abducted—into rebel militias and military groups. The long-term emotional and physical damage the child soldiers endure during their military service makes the rebuilding of their shattered lives extremely complicated. Some have seen their friends and family killed, or even been forced to kill loved ones in order to stay alive. Some children, especially those who have injured or killed people in their communities, believe they cannot ever return to their former lives and homes.

At the beginning of 2000, it was estimated that some 120,000 child soldiers were being used throughout Africa, which amounts to one third of the world's total. In recent years, as some longstanding conflicts have ended, many child soldiers have been released from service, but an estimated 100,000 are believed to remain. Some countries directly support using children under the age of 18 as soldiers in their militaries, while other nations indirectly support the practice by accepting support from militia and paramilitary forces that recruit and employ children in war zones.

Detecting and destroying land mines from Angola's civil war. A worker employed by the charity organization HALO Trust, which specializes in removing debris left behind after warfare, searches the area around the village of Liambanbo in this July 2005 photograph.

At the international level, the use of child soldiers has been outlawed by a number of treaties. For example, the United Nations Optional Protocol to the Convention on the Rights of the Child considers the direct use of children under the age of 18 in wars and conflict, or their compulsory recruitment, to be illegal. The International Criminal Court defines the recruitment of

A child soldier of the Sudan People's Liberation Army before his demobilization in July 2000. In 2004 the Coalition to Stop the Use of Child Soldiers reported that an estimated 100,000 children were involved in large-scale conflicts in countries such as Burundi, Cote d'Ivoire, the Democratic Republic of the Congo, Somalia, Sudan, and Uganda.

children under the age of 15 as a war crime, and most regional organizations, including the European Union and the African Union, condemn the practice.

Many UN aid groups and organizations, with the help of international and local NGOs, use "demobilization, disarmament, and reintegration," or DDR, as the steps to build peace in war-torn regions. Through DDR programs, for example, UNICEF helps former child soldiers obtain new skills and reintegrate into their communities.

In an effort to share how being a child soldier had affected his life, Alhaji Babah Sawaneh, of Sierra Leone, appeared before the UN Security Council in 2001. He explained:

> When I was 10 years old ... my elder brother and I ... ran into the rebels. We were taken back to our village where we were tied up,

beaten and kept in the hot burning sun. Many houses were burnt down and people killed. My uncle was later killed.... we were trained for a week to shoot and dismantle AK47 guns. Thereafter I was used to fighting. We killed people, burnt down houses, destroyed properties and cut limbs. But most of the time I went on food raids and did domestic work for my commander's wife....

In January 2000, two years after my capture, UN peacekeepers met with our commander to explain the DDR process. Within two days more than 250 children were released. We were taken to a care centre in Lunsar and I was later handed over to [the local nongovernmental organization] Caritas Makeni for care and protection.

Despite UN efforts to eliminate the use of child soldiers, the practice persists, even in countries that signed on to treaties barring it. The Coalition to Stop the Use of Child Soldiers, a group made up of international NGOs such as Amnesty International and Human Rights Watch, remains concerned that DDR programs often lack sufficient funds and resources to be effective.

TRUTH AND RECONCILIATION COMMISSIONS

Some peacebuilding efforts involve establishing ways for factions to apologize for, be forgiven for, or come to terms with past violence. Truth and reconciliation commissions, which often receive funds and technical expertise from NGOs and governmental groups, provide such forums. Truth commissions publicly address and document issues of human rights violations and war crimes, in attempts to determine what happened and who was responsible. They may even include provisions for amnesty, forgiveness, or appropriate justice. Victims get the chance to be heard and perpetrators have the opportunity to apologize and request the opportunity to reintegrate back into society. South Africa, Sierra Leone, Rwanda, the Central African Republic, Ghana, Nigeria, and Kenya have all sponsored truth commissions. Other countries exploring the option of this forum are Liberia and the Democratic Republic of the Congo.

In Sierra Leone, a truth and reconciliation commission began hearings in 2003 to deal with the aftermath of a decade of bloody civil war. Funded through and coordinated by the UN Office of the High Commissioner for Human Rights, the Sierra Leone Truth and Reconciliation Commission also received consulting assistance from the International Center for Transitional Justice. Thousands of statements were received from victims and perpetrators, and hundreds testified publicly. However, in a nation with tens of thousands of perpetrators, and multiple gruesome crimes, the effectiveness of the commission in addressing the various issues has been questioned.

Dealing with conflicts requires both preventative measures and rebuilding after a conflict has ended. Poor countries are

During the 1990s, the rebel group Revolutionary United Front waged a campaign of terror in Sierra Leone, during which thousands were killed, raped, or mutilated. The young girl shown here had both hands cut off. The Sierra Leone Truth and Reconciliation Commission, funded in part by nongovernmental organizations, has helped bring atrocities to light in an effort to bring peace to the tortured country.

often starved of resources, and so there are a number of areas where the international community can assist. The Commission for Africa report *Our Common Interest* suggested that donor nations can improve the effectiveness of aid by recognizing the importance of a healthy economy in preventing conflict. The report stressed that rich countries' aid should go to promote economic development and fair trade, because these issues fuel conflicts. Post-conflict financing could also be addressed, the Commission noted, by helping developing countries that have fallen behind in payments clear arrears so they are creditworthy and able to obtain future concessional financing for rebuilding.

SMALL ARMS TRAFFICKING

A threat to peace and security of African nations is the easy access to small arms, which are both imported and manufactured locally. After the end of the Cold War, in 1991, the number of civil wars and ethnic conflicts in Africa increased significantly. They commonly featured the use of small arms and light weapons (such as guns, mortars, landmines, grenades, and light missiles). While exact numbers are difficult to come by, it is generally accepted that these weapons are responsible for some 60 to 90 percent of deaths in Africa, depending on the conflict.

Small arms and light weapons destabilize regions throughout the world, says the United Nations Department for Disarmament Affairs. They spark, fuel, and prolong conflicts; obstruct relief programs; undermine peace initiatives; exacerbate human rights abuses; hamper development; and foster a culture of violence.

Small arms are easy to conceal, and easy to maintain. Because they are mass-produced, they are cheap and easily available. There are an estimated 500 million small arms in the world today, says Robert Neild in the book *Public Corruption: The Dark Side of Social Evolution.* Guns are cheap in Africa, he noted: "In

1999 it was reported that an AK-47 assault rifle could be bought in Uganda for the price of a chicken."

Toward the end of the 1990s, recognizing the role that small arms play in fueling conflicts, the international community took up the issue. Although South Africa had been a major small arms producer, contributing to numerous conflicts in southern Africa, the country announced in 1999 its commitment to combating the flow of small arms to civil wars and ethnic conflicts. The same year, the UN Security Council discussed the issue for the first time, and passed a resolution to take action against the scourge of small arms.

Africa's natural resources, particularly diamonds and oil, have been used to create an "economy of war" in many nations of the continent. Militias and rebel groups assume power over regions rich in diamonds, oil, or narcotics, and sell them to fund the purchases of small arms and supplies. For example, diamonds have come to U.S. and European markets from rebel-controlled areas of Angola and Sierra Leone, with the proceeds being used to fund rebel armies and militia. Similarly, the mineral coltan, which is used in computers and cell phones, is sold to fund rebel militias in Rwanda, Uganda, and the Democratic Republic of the Congo. As global demand for coltan has grown, rebel groups have increased their mining operations to help finance civil wars.

There is a lack of international consensus on the small arms trade issue. Stemming the flow of small arms and light weapons is difficult because in many countries these weapons are seen as legitimate, and necessary for law enforcement, military purposes, and even sport or recreational use. In the United States, for example, many consider gun ownership to be a fundamental right.

In 2001, at the UN Conference on the Illicit Trade in Small Arms and Light Weapons, numerous countries (including the United States, China, and South Africa) refused to limit sales of

In an effort to reduce the number of illegal firearms, South African police destroy a collection of more than 1,000 weapons in September 2003. While the United Nations does not favor a global gun ban, United Nations Secretary-General Kofi Annan says, the organization has worked since 2001 to develop a consensus among the international community over "effective enforcement, better controls and regulation, safer stockpiling, and weapons collection and destruction" of firearms. UN efforts have led to toughened laws in 50 countries against illegal guns and their destruction in 60 nations.

small arms to countries that were at risk of using them to violate human rights or for warfare. The United States did not support the idea of restricting civilian possession of small arms, or of placing any restrictions on the legal manufacture and trade of small arms weapons.

However, UN member states did agree to establishing systems for collecting and destroying illegal weapons, adopting and/or improving national legislations that would help criminalize the illicit trade in small arms, and creating strict import and export controls. Some NGOs have criticized the final plan as being too weak, for providing no international mechanism for monitoring compliance, and for limiting the UN's role to compiling information submitted by states on a voluntary basis.

Despite the lack of progress in establishing stronger international restrictions on the small arms trade, African countries and international NGOs continue to lobby for change. In addition to being involved in initiatives to prevent the misuse and illegal trade of small arms, many state and nongovernmental organizations have addressed their threat in post-conflict regions by establishing programs that encourage the handing in of weapons and destruction of arms stockpiles.

HELPING AFRICA HELP ITSELF

When applied successfully, foreign aid delivery and debt relief for impoverished nations can help increase educational opportunities, open access to health services, promote economic growth and stability, and assist in conflict prevention and post-conflict rebuilding. The international community has much to gain by lifting the developing nations of Africa out of poverty and into the economic marketplace.

PROVIDING MORE AID

Some economists believe that the aid being given to Africa has been too little, and of poor quality for too long. If developing countries had received all of the aid promised since the early 1970s—an estimated $2.5 trillion—they would have had more resources to deal with poverty.

Public pressure to do more to help developing countries has grown in recent years as individuals and organizations of donor countries have held rallies at official meetings and at benefit

Performers at the Live 8 concert near Tokyo, Japan. Ten Live 8 concerts were held in July 2005 just before the G8 summit. Organizers of the events hoped to educate the public about poverty in Africa and pressure leaders of wealthy nations to agree to debt cancellation, establishment of fair world trade practices, and giving of additional foreign aid.

performances, urging their public leaders to take action. In 2005, just before the Gleneagles G8 summit meeting, hundreds of thousands attended Live 8 concerts, which called on the heads of the world's richest countries to end poverty and forgive debt in developing countries.

Activist rock star Bono, of the band U2, has helped lead the call for Western nations to help Africa. His lobbying group, DATA (which stands for Debt, AIDS, Trade, Africa), issued a statement in June 2006 commending industrialized nations for following through on their promises made at Gleneagles, by having officially canceled the debts of 19 of the 40 eligible poor countries. This debt forgiveness, DATA reported, meant that the countries of Cameroon, Mozambique, Tanzania, Uganda, and

Zambia would be able to more fully fund public health and education programs.

However, DATA also noted that much more remains to be done. For example, funding to fight HIV/AIDS grew from $300 million in the late 1990s to $8.3 billion in 2005—support that enabled 700,000 more HIV/AIDS patients in Africa to receive antiretroviral treatment (up from 100,000 in 2003). However, this number is still far short of the goal to provide AIDS treatment to at least 4 million Africans by 2010. DATA also admonished wealthy nations for missing targets that would ensure the full $50 billion of promised aid will be delivered to developing countries by the target date of 2010. To do so, its report noted, rich countries should have given $3.6 billion in 2005, but gave only $1.6 billion.

MAKING AID MORE EFFECTIVE

The reason many donor countries place conditions on aid delivery and debt relief is because of the region's history of corruption and misuse of aid. Sometimes these conditions can be positive, such as when governments are required to clamp down on corruption, strengthen transparency, or improve the quality of democracy. However, when conditional aid has required economic reforms—such as liberalization of the economy—such policies can be harmful. Aid can also be ineffective when it is "tied"—a practice that typically reduces the value of the contribution.

Activist and lead singer of the band U2, Bono announces the formation of Debt, AIDS, Trade, Africa (DATA), at the World Economic Forum in New York, in 2002. "We have an agenda," he said at the time, "which we're calling the 'DATA Agenda': 'Debt, AIDS and trade for Africa, in return for democracy, accountability and transparency in Africa.'"

Aid has been shown to be more effective when governments operate in open political environments, in which officials must be accountable for how money is used. Inadequate administrative and political institutions have been the source of inequality, corruption, human rights abuses, and conflicts in Africa. However, in recent years, the African people have begun to address the lack of good governance, as nations have come to terms with internal problems. Beginning in the mid-1990s highly publicized political scandals have rocked South Africa and a few East Africa nations. However, the fact that the media in those countries could report on such corruption shows that their governments have become more open. Nevertheless, many poor countries still need to tackle corruption and improve transparency of government.

Some analysts believe that the growing number of democracies in Africa is a sign of positive political reform across the continent. In the 1980s, only five African countries (Botswana, Gambia, Mauritius, Senegal, and Zimbabwe) held competitive elections. That number rose dramatically during the 1990s, when 40 African countries held multiparty elections that, according to international observers, were free and fair. African countries slowly appear to be moving toward democracy and openness.

Aid and debt relief has also been shown to be more effective in countries with growing economies and reduced poverty. A number of African nations have seen improvements in their economy, the IMF reported in 2005, when it noted that 25 nations, representing three quarters of Africa's population, were showing steady economic improvement. The past 10 years have seen growth rates of 4 percent in 16 African countries, the IMF also reported.

A 2005 OECD report has estimated that economic activity in Africa would reach nearly 5 percent and predicted growth rates

At a 2003 UN meeting on HIV/AIDS, African states could report having made little progress in achieving the Millennium Development Goal of reducing disease prevalence.

of 5.8 percent in 2006 and 5.5 percent in 2007. However much of this rise is coming from oil-exporting nations such as Nigeria, Angola, and countries in central and in southern Africa.

Unfortunately economic improvements remain slow in sub-Saharan Africa, where it is unlikely that the region will be able meet the UN Millennium Goal of raising half of its poor out of poverty by 2015. An additional concern is the impact of problems like AIDS, which threatens to overwhelm economic progress in many African countries.

PROVIDING ADDITIONAL DEBT RELIEF

Debt relief has the potential to be more useful than aid. It targets the poorest countries, although other countries not as poor but

In April 1994 millions of South Africans stood in long lines to vote in their country's first multiracial elections, subsequently electing Nelson Mandela as president. The increase in the number of democratic elections taking place in Africa encourages many Western leaders, who believe strong African leadership and good governance are essential to ending poverty in Africa.

also burdened with high debt may benefit from relief, too. To repay massive debts, countries cut budgets and raise taxes, creating an unhealthy economic environment for investment. Debt write-off eliminates the need for such austerity measures and frees up resources that governments can use to address issues of poverty, disease, and humanitarian crises.

However, there have been problems with debt relief. Promises of large quantities of aid or debt write-off for the poorest nations have sometimes been accompanied by delays in fulfillment. In certain cases the debt cancellation process may cover the span of several years. The $40 billion in debt relief promised at the

Gleneagles summit, for example, is being given over the course of 40 years, or effectively $1 billion per year.

In other cases, the promised amount of foreign aid is less than what was expected, often because it includes previously earmarked money. At Gleneagles, public leaders announced they were doubling the amount of promised aid from $25 billion to $50 billion by 2010, but the increase was actually around $15 to $20 billion; the rest had been promised earlier. In addition, debt write-off may be contingent on harsh economic conditions. Critics of the Gleneagles debt relief note that for every dollar written off, a dollar of future aid would be withheld. In other words, the African countries that will receive this promised aid will have to forgo future developmental aid.

PROVIDING FAIRER INTERNATIONAL TRADE

Imbalances in trade polices have left many developing countries vulnerable in a global economy. The use of agricultural subsidies by wealthy nations and the restrictions on generic AIDS drugs are issues that affect the survival of millions in Africa.

Anti-poverty activists believe that the influential members of the international community can assist Africa by ensuring that international trade is fairer to developing countries. By removing tariffs and opening their markets to African goods, developed nations can give poor countries the tools to help Africa. Although the leaders of industrialized countries have acknowledged that world trade policies favor the wealthy countries, efforts to change those rules through the Doha trade talks have failed.

USING A COMMUNITY-BASED APPROACH

Organizations working in Africa and other parts of the world have long highlighted the need to empower local people so

they may be better prepared to climb out of poverty themselves. In a community-based approach, projects are carried
out in consultation with local and national government officials. Many national and international NGOs support CBOs,
or community-based organizations—initiatives started by
members of communities to address specific problems afflicting their region.

NGOs may work with CBOs in partnerships, by providing
developmental aid, services, or technical assistance. For example,
the NGO African Solutions to African Problems (ASAP) provides support to various CBOs running drop-in centers, schools,
and early childhood development centers that provide nutrition,
education, and medical support for children affected by

Children from the Baphumelele children's home in Khayelitsha, near Cape Town, South Africa, pose in
November 2003 with rock star Bono and singer Beyonce Knowles, before their performance at an anti-
AIDS concert. The community-based organization Baphumelele was founded by local resident Rosalia
Mashale to help children in her area who have been abandoned or orphaned because of HIV/AIDS.

HIV/AIDS. Among the CBOs sponsored by ASAP are two in South Africa—Baphumelele, a daycare program in the township of Khayelitsha, and the Zwelitsha Youth Farm Project, in which youth raise and sell produce, with the proceeds used to support the education of AIDS orphans.

Economist William Easterly argues that donor-led programs, such as the Structural Adjustment Programme, Millennium Development Goals, and other large-scale projects impose conditions in a top-down, "West-knows-best" approach. In *The White Man's Burden*, he states that this top-down approach of "large international bureaucracies giving aid to large national government bureaucracies . . . is not getting money to the poor." With top-down programs, he complains, the donor is in charge of aid delivery, and the recipients do not have any input into programs. As a result, there is a lack of effective feedback, evaluation, and ultimately accountability in aid programs since agencies do not need to find out what works and what the poor actually need and want.

Easterly advises donors to not try to transform governments or societies, but instead focus on helping individuals. He says donors need to "put the focus back where it belongs":

> [G]et the poorest people in the world such obvious goods as the vaccines, the antibiotics, the food supplements, the improved seeds, the fertilizers, the roads, the boreholes, the water pipes, the textbooks, and the nurses. This is not making the poor dependent on handouts; it is giving the poorest people the health, nutrition, and education, and other inputs that raise the payoff to their own efforts to better their lives.

PROMOTING SELF-SUFFICIENCY

Some critics of foreign aid see it as a cause of rather than solution to Africa's problems. They believe that the availability of foreign aid promotes dependency, irresponsible borrowing, and hinders necessary reforms. Similarly, they say, debt relief encourages borrowers to continue borrowing, in the expectation that they can take on new loans that eventually will also be forgiven.

In July 2006 Oxfam issued the report *Causing Hunger: An Overview of the Food Crisis in Africa*, in which the humanitarian organization acknowledged that regular donations of food aid have failed Africa, because the causes of hunger crises in Africa were not being dealt with. The report noted that despite the efforts of Oxfam, other NGOs, and governments the average number of food emergencies in Africa per year had almost tripled since the mid-1980s. In addition, the Oxfam report noted, delivery of food aid took as long as five months, because most of it came from overseas, and typically cost up to 50 percent more than locally purchased goods.

Aid to Africa has not focused enough on development programs, Oxfam says. Between 1997 and 2003, humanitarian assistance to Africa rose from $946 million to more than $3 billion. During this time of increase in aid to sub-Saharan Africa, there was a 43 percent decrease in agricultural production aid, which fell from $1.7 billion (1990–1992) to $974 million (2000–2002). The Oxfam report states that aid should be encouraging people to learn ways to take care of themselves. It recommends that in times of food crises the international community should be spending aid money on foods produced by local farmers—and not paying farmers in the developed world for surplus food commodities sent to Africa as aid.

Some economists do not believe the international community should be giving aid at all to developing countries because it does not support growth. Others argue that many African countries do not have the financial or technical resources to effectively develop on their own. Today, more than half of all African governments get about 50 percent of the revenue for their annual budgets from foreign aid.

A worker from the USAID-sponsored program Digital Freedom Initiative (left) explains how a Senegalese clothing merchant can use computer technology in his business. The goal of the USAID program is to promote economic growth by sharing information and communication technology with business owners in developing countries.

INVESTING IN AFRICA

Africans investing in African businesses is a better alternative to foreign aid and debt relief says Center for Global Development president Nancy Birdsall and coauthors in a July/August 2005 article in the journal *Foreign Affairs*. "The contrasting experiences of eastern Asia, China, and India suggest that the secret of poverty-reducing growth lies in creating business opportunities for domestic investors, including the poor," they write.

In his book *Economic Democracy: The Political Struggle of the 21st Century*, J. W. Smith suggests that foreign investors can also help Africans—but not by giving cash. To avoid the channeling of development aid to private bank accounts and other misuse of aid that occurs in corrupt governments, he says, investors should build the actual industry:

> To build a balanced economy, provide consumer buying power, and develop arteries of commerce that will absorb the production of these industries, contractors and labor in those countries should be used. Legitimacy and security of contracts is the basis of any sound economy. Engineers know what those costs should be and, if cost overruns start coming in, the contractor who has proven incapable should be replaced—just as any good contract would require.

Fear of corruption is not the only reason for the lack of investment in Africa. Many foreign firms shy away because of the continent's image as a poverty-stricken land. Some people criticize humanitarian agencies and the media for perpetuating the image of Africa as a land in crisis. As a result, all African countries—no matter how economically sound—are negatively branded, and less likely to be considered for outside investment.

AFRICA'S FUTURE

Africa continues to face many challenges that can undermine growth: HIV/AIDS; underfunded health and educational systems; drought and food crises in eastern, western, and southern African countries; and inadequate communication, transportation, and institutional infrastructures. In addition, conflicts and political unrest in Ethiopia, Côte d'Ivoire, the Democratic Republic of the Congo, and the oil-rich delta region of Nigeria also threaten to hinder economic growth prospects.

Pressure on world leaders to provide extra debt relief to the poorest nations, to commit to fairer trade, and to improve aid quality has led to economic and political improvements in some

African countries. However much more needs to be done. The delivery of predictable, adequate funding can help the impoverished nations of Africa achieve economic progress and social stability. However, empowered African leadership—at community, local, and national levels—will be key to the success of Africa in overcoming its many challenges.

GLOSSARY

COMMUNITY-BASED ORGANIZATION (CBO)—an NGO that serves a specific population in a small geographical area.

COMPULSORY LICENSING—a provision in the WTO's global trade rules that allows a developing country to force a patent holders to grant a domestic manufacturer or other country the right to produce the product.

DEVELOPING NATION—a country with a low per-capita income and access to few goods and services.

DEVELOPMENT ASSISTANCE COMMITTEE (DAC)—specialized committee of the Organization for Economic Cooperation and Development that is made up of industrialized, wealthy countries.

ECONOMIC GLOBALIZATION—the worldwide interdependence among countries connected through the selling of goods and services.

FOREIGN AID—assistance given to other countries; the term is often used to describe aid given by rich countries of the OECD to developing nations.

GENERIC DRUGS—low-priced, biologically equivalent alternatives to brand-name, patented drugs.

INTERNATIONAL NGO—nongovernmental organization that operates programs in more than one country.

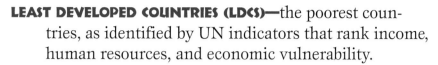

LEAST DEVELOPED COUNTRIES (LDCS)—the poorest countries, as identified by UN indicators that rank income, human resources, and economic vulnerability.

MILLENNIUM DEVELOPMENT GOALS (MDGS)—goals agreed to by the governments of UN member states to halve world poverty and hunger, protect the environment, improve health and sanitation, address discrimination against women, and reduce illiteracy.

NATIONAL NGO—nongovernmental organization that operates within an individual country.

NEOLIBERALISM—a mostly economic ideology that encourages development through policies that require cuts in state expenditure, the opening of markets to foreign competition and investment, and the privatization of many state functions and assets.

NONGOVERNMENTAL ORGANIZATION (NGO)—nonprofit groups or associations operating outside the government; they include charities and research institutions, civil society organizations, and groups working to address social, economic, environmental, political, and other issues.

ODIOUS DEBT—money owed by a developing country that was loaned to a previous government, even though the creditor knew the funds would be used for purposes counter to the interests of the nation.

OFFICIAL DEVELOPMENT ASSISTANCE (ODA)—foreign aid given by donor nations to poor countries to promote economic and social development; members of the DAC have agreed to give 0.7 percent of their gross national income (GNI) as ODA.

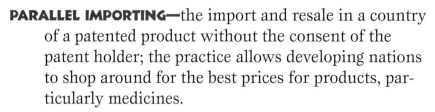

GLOSSARY

PARALLEL IMPORTING—the import and resale in a country of a patented product without the consent of the patent holder; the practice allows developing nations to shop around for the best prices for products, particularly medicines.

PATENT—the exclusive right given to the inventor or maker of a product to produce, use, or sell that item.

STRUCTURAL ADJUSTMENT PROGRAMME (SAP)—a set of economic policies designed to correct imbalances in trade and government budgets; the policies typically include increasing privatization, opening national markets for foreign competition, and reducing government spending.

THIRD WORLD DEBT—money owed by developing nations due to heavy borrowing and high interest rates.

TRADE-RELATED ASPECTS OF INTELLECTUAL PROPERTY (TRIPS)—patent rules as defined by the World Trade Organization (WTO).

USER FEES—charges for services such as health care, which are paid for by the user at the time of service.

FURTHER READING

Bello, Walden. *Dark Victory: The United States and Global Poverty*. Oakland, CA: Food First/Institute for Food and Development Policy, 1999.

Chang, Ha-Joon. *Kicking Away the Ladder*. London: Anthem Press, 2002.

Commission for Africa. *Our Common Interest: Report of the Commission for Africa*. March 2005. http://www.commissionforafrica.org/english/report/introduction.html

Easterly, William, *The White Man's Burden: Why the West's Efforts to Aid the Rest Have Done So Much Ill and So Little Good*. New York: Penguin Press, 2006.

Robbins, Richard H. *Global Problems and the Culture of Capitalism*. Allyn & Bacon, 2005.

Smith, J. W. *Economic Democracy: The Political Struggle of the 21st Century*, Radford, VA: Institute for Economic Democracy Press, 2005.

Stiglitz, Joseph. *Globalization and Its Discontents*, New York: W. W. Norton & Company, 2003.

Van de Walle, Nicolas, *African Economies and the Politics of Permanent Crisis, 1979–1999*. Cambridge: Cambridge University Press, 2001.

INTERNET RESOURCES

HTTP://WWW.GLOBALISSUES.ORG

The author's website, where global issues of poverty, Africa, and more are discussed.

HTTP://WWW.OECD.ORG

The website for the Organization for Economic Cooperation and Development, which contains links to statistics on Official Development Assistance aid donated by member DAC countries.

HTTP://WWW.OXFAM.ORG

The website for the NGO Oxfam, which campaigns on issues related to Africa, poverty, third world debt, trade, development, and more.

HTTP://WWW.AFRICAACTION.ORG

Africa Action is one of the oldest organizations in the United States working on issues concerned with Africa, in particular the relationship with the United States.

HTTP://WWW.ALLAFRICA.COM

An African-based news site with sources from over 300 organizations, including many news organizations throughout the continent.

HTTP://WWW.TRANSPARENCY.ORG

The website for Transparency International, a leading campaign organization that fights global corruption.

HTTP://WWW.WORLDBANK.ORG

The World Bank official website provides loans and grants to promote economic development; source for *World Development Report 2006*.

HTTP://WWW.IMF.ORG

The official website of the International Monetary Fund; contains information on the history of the organization and its activities to promote global economic growth and stability.

HTTP://WWW.UN.ORG

The United Nations official website contains links to UN Millennium Development Goals, news about current global issues, and background information on the organization.

HTTP://WWW.WHO.INT

An agency of the United Nations, the World Health Organization monitors diseases around the world and works in partnerships with global health initiatives to save lives. Its website includes links to health information and statistics by country.

HTTP://WWW.UNAIDS.ORG

The Joint United Nations Programme on HIV/AIDS official website links to regional information on the disease in sub-Saharan Africa.

HTTP://WWW.CGDEV.ORG

The Center for Global Development website features links to research on development challenges to Africa; includes the report *Millions Saved: Proven Successes in Global Health,* which describes effective health initiatives in the developing world.

Publisher's Note: The websites listed on this page were active at the time of publication. The publisher is not responsible for websites that have changed their address or discontinued operation since the date of publication. The publisher will review and update the websites each time the book is reprinted.

INDEX

Numbers in ***bold italic*** refer to captions.

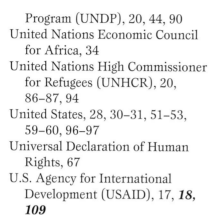

PICTURE CREDITS

CONTRIBUTORS

PROFESSOR ROBERT I. ROTBERG is Director of the Program on Intrastate Conflict and Conflict Resolution at the Kennedy School, Harvard University, and President of the World Peace Foundation. He is the author of a number of books and articles on Africa, including *A Political History of Tropical Africa* and *Ending Autocracy, Enabling Democracy: The Tribulations of Southern Africa*.

ANUP SHAH, born in 1974 in the United Kingdom, has been reading and writing about global issues since 1998. He has written articles for various publications around the world, and appeared on some radio interviews. He started the globalissues.org website in mid-1998 in his spare time while living in the United States, in an effort to show how most global issues are interrelated. The site has over 550 articles, mostly written by the author, and currently receives up to 50,000 page views daily. GlobalIssues.org is a partner site of the www.oneworld.net and www.mediachannel.org.